MW00339906

Boone and Crockett Club's Complete Guide to

Hunting Whitetails

Deer Hunting Tips Guaranteed to Improve Your Success in the Field

Informative Chapters by

René R. Barrientos, Craig Boddington, Richard Hale, Ken Hayworth, Jay Lesser, Jack Reneau, Dave Richards, Glen Salow, Justin Spring, Larry Weishuhn, Bill Winke, and Gordon Whittington

Measuring Illustrations by

Dallen Lambson

A BOONE AND CROCKETT CLUB PUBLICATION

Missoula, Montana I 2014

Boone and Crockett Club's Complete Guide to Hunting Whitetails

Contributing authors include René Barrientos,
Craig Boddington, Al Brothers, Richard Hale,
Ken Hayworth, Jay Lesser, Wm. H. Nesbitt,
Jack Reneau, Dave Richards, Glen Salow,
Justin Spring, Larry Weishuhn, Bill Winke,
Gordon Whittington, and Philip L. Wright.

Library of Congress Catalog Card Number: 2014940497
Paperback ISBN: 978-1-940860-00-8
Published July 2014

Published in the United States of America by the
Boone and Crockett Club
250 Station Drive, Missoula, Montana 59801
Phone (406) 542-1888
Fax (406) 542-0784
Toll-Free (888) 840-4868 (book orders only)
www.boone-crockett.org

"The whitetail is the most beautiful and graceful of all our big game animals when in motion."

Theodore Roosevelt
The Deer Family
part of the American Sportsmen's Library

Boone and Crockett Club Mission Statement

It is the mission of the Boone and Crockett Club to promote the conservation and management of wildlife, especially big game, and its habitat, to preserve and encourage hunting and to maintain the highest ethical standards of fair chase and sportsmanship in North America.

TO LEARN MORE ABOUT B&C VISIT WWW.BOONE-CROCKETT.ORG

Contents

Use wind and rain to your advantage when setting up your stand/blind after you've identified the buck you are after. Find more information on trail-cam use in the tactics chapter starting on **Page 108**.

Note how the shoulder bones obstruct much of the heart/lung area in a quartering-on shot. Learn more in Boddington's chapter on the Perfect Shot on **Page 64**.

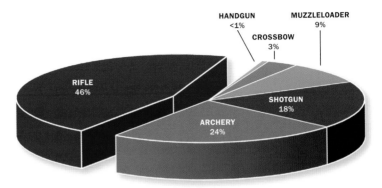

Did you know B&C accepts archery, shotgun, and other methods of harvest in our records book? More than half of our hunter-taken whitetail entries are **not** harvested with a rifle. Turn to **Page 202** for more statistics about trophy whitetail deer.

Foreword

GOD BLESS THE WHITETAIL DEER! FROM REMNANT populations just a century ago, his tribe has prospered to become the most numerous big game animal on planet Earth, now numbering somewhere above 30 million. The recovery of the whitetail deer is one of North America's finest conservation legends. But that's only part of the story. The rest is that the whitetail deer has created, fostered—and now supports—the greatest hunting culture in the world.

According to U.S. Fish and Wildlife's most recent survey, America registers some 16 million hunters. This is not the largest per-capita percentage of hunters in the world; that honor probably goes to Finland. However, if we add hunters from Canada and Mexico and factor in Americans who, by age or other status, are not required to purchase annual hunting licenses and thus cannot be counted in any survey, North America has closer to 20 million hunters. This is a large hunting public, by millions far beyond what any other continent can muster.

I am a traveling hunter, for whatever reason innately compelled to ramp distant horizons. But I am very much in the minority. The same surveys that give us an approximate number of hunters consistently suggest that the vast majority of hunters pursue their sport close to home, with only a small fraction ever venturing outside of their home states. This is fact. A logical but rational extension is that we hunt because it is part of who and what we are, and we are most likely to pursue the game that is most available and most accessible in our own backyards.

Once again, God bless the whitetail deer! Unlike the majority of our North American big game species, the whitetail deer has learned not only to survive, but to thrive, in proximity with man. A creature of the edge, he loves the mosaic of agriculture and woodlot. A clever animal, survivors

Boddington's 2012 Kansas buck is the best taken from his Kansas farm to date. Every year he has seen larger bucks, but this buck is getting close to the area's potential.

9

of his kind persisted through relentless persecution in the 18th and 19th centuries. Given a bit of protection, he prospered in the early years of the 20th century, and in the latter half, as sometimes happens with animal populations, he exploded. Today, one subspecies or another of whitetail deer is both huntable and hunted in 46 states of the Lower 48, in all provinces of Canada and most of Mexico.

The whitetail deer has become the most democratic of all game animals, available on lands private and public almost throughout North America. In much of the United States he is a pest to agriculture, and according to insurance companies, one of the greatest road hazards. The management imperative to hunt the whitetail deer is probably stronger than for any other animal on Earth. North America's hunters have responded. Today more than 10 million North Americans consider themselves, by avocation, deer hunters—even though they can only pursue their hobby during a narrow window of open seasons.

Many of us hunters are specialists: turkey hunters, elk hunters, sheep hunters, waterfowl hunters, upland game hunters. Some of us follow all the seasons. But, continent-wide, the largest group of all, and the largest group in the world, is the North American deer hunters. The whitetail deer has spawned not only the world's largest hunting culture but also the world's largest hunting industry. Deer scents, deer calls, camouflage, decoys, lures, tree stands, ground blinds, and so much more, all produced and consumed just to increase the odds to take a whitetail deer. The products available to the whitetail deer hunter—now including this most valuable book—are legion. And this has all happened well within living memory.

Hunters younger than I may not recall a time when there were few or no deer, but let's take my home state of Kansas as a microcosm. Today we know Kansas to be a great destination for whitetail deer. It is so good today that it's easy to forget that deer were declared extinct by 1925. During World War II a few started to filter in from neighboring states. But when I was a kid in the late 1950s there were still very few deer in Kansas, and there was certainly no deer hunting. The first modern season, in 1964, was a historic event—but tags were few and hunter interest modest.

In those days, Kansas hunters were upland bird hunters; ownership of a deer rifle was rare. As farming practices changed and new reservoirs filled, many of my Kansas hunting buddies—following the principle of hunting the game most available and most accessible close to home—became

Boddington and Zack Aultman with a great Georgia whitetail. This is not Boddington's highest-scoring buck, but coming from the Southeast he considers it his best.

waterfowl hunters. And then, well after the first modern season, the deer herd exploded. Today the quail hunting buddies of my youth are hunters of the whitetail deer. Kansas now sells something over 180,000 deer licenses annually, a rather far cry from exactly zero just 40 years ago!

Kansas, the last state to open a modern deer season, is just a small example. It happened at different times in different places, but through the 60s and into the 70s the long-nurtured whitetail deer populations exploded all across America. This created hunting opportunity, which bred new hunters and spawned almost a cult of hunting the whitetail deer. This continues to this day, witnessed by this very book, but just 40 years ago the interest in whitetail deer was limited and localized.

As a young writer and editor I was fortunate to have a number of mentors, but few were as kind or generous as John Wootters, who passed on to better deer stands just a year ago. John was a Texan, and as such his deer hunting was...*different*...from that of the deer hunters in the East, Southeast, and upper Midwest. Even so, his 1975 work, *Hunting Trophy Deer*, was a landmark on the subject. Amazingly and wildly successful, it was probably the very first book that focused on hunting mature, trophy-class bucks. To a great extent, *Hunting Trophy Deer* launched what we think of today as the "whitetail cult." At that time, Wootters was writing for *Petersen's Hunting* magazine, which I would shortly join. He implored then-editor Ken Elliott to write a column strictly on deer hunting, primarily the whitetail deer. Elliott was skeptical, as I would have been in the 1970s: "Do you really think enough people would actually read a column just on deer hunting?"

Fortunately for us all, Wootters won the argument. His "Buck Sense" column was perennially the most popular column in the magazine—also the longest running, continuing through my 14-year tenure as editor—only ending when Wootters, the original "Mr. Whitetail," retired in the late 1990s. Yes, there is serious interest in hunting the whitetail deer, without question more serious—almost fanatical—interest than surrounds any other game animal in the world. Serious hunters of the whitetail deer will try almost anything to get a better crack at a trophy buck!

Obviously "trophy" is in the mind of the beholder. The holy grail is a whitetail buck that achieves the Boone and Crockett All-time minimum score of 170 (net, typical). Such a buck is just a handful of every million bucks harvested. Although the taking of such a buck ranks high on my own bucket list, I freely admit that I have never taken one. I share this lack with the vast majority of America's deer hunters, and like them, it is unlikely that I ever will. The odds are not favorable.

Unlike many hunters, however, I can say with reasonable certainty that I have actually seen such a buck. It was in the Swan Valley of Montana, twenty-some years ago. Ed Nixon and I were standing on a ridge, and we saw a buck cross a clearcut into a patch of timber far below. And what a buck! He was a typical 12-point, massive beams well outside his ears. It is impossible to accurately judge an animal that is exponentially larger than one has ever seen before, so I won't put a number on him (although I still have a number in my mind's eye), but be assured he was big. And by our thinking, he was ours. We made a quick plan, executed a small drive, and each of us expected to see the buck or hear a shot. The buck thought differently; he slipped out the back side and, to my knowledge, was never seen again.

That's the way it is with whitetail deer. Antler size depends on food, minerals, genetics, and age. A great buck in one area may be an average buck in another (and vice versa), but the whitetail deer is not only the most populous, but as such is also the hardest-hunted animal on Earth. A buck that has survived several hunting seasons and lived to grow the maximum antlers that his habitat and lineage allow is arguably the most difficult animal in the world to bring to bag. A mature whitetail is like a ghost, largely nocturnal and incredibly canny. It isn't important that a whitetail buck reach our Boone and Crockett minimum, because most never will. In some hard-hunted areas, realistically, any whitetail deer is a trophy, and any buck is a great trophy. Anywhere, by definition, a mature whitetail buck is an awesome trophy. Some hunters are more skilled than others, and some are also luckier than others. But a hunter who has achieved even occasionally consistent success on mature whitetail bucks should be considered among the world's greatest hunters.

By both vocation and avocation I have been incredibly fortunate to have hunted much of the world's great game country and much of the world's great game. I am often asked about my favorite hunt or game animal. It's a hard question, because I truly love it all. But at some point we all come down to our roots. Like so many millions of North American hunters, at heart I am a hunter of the whitetail deer. He is more frustrating than bongo, more challenging than buffalo, and so much warier than any wild sheep that ever lived! Returning to my roots, I've had a little farm in Kansas for some years now where I can match wits with the whitetail deer on my own terms—and on his. Every summer and early fall I see major bucks that we never quite seem to see when deer season rolls around. So the deer are winning but only for now. One of these days one of my big bucks will make a mistake, and I'll be there to capitalize. Or at least that's the way I see it in my dreams. And in the meantime, along with you, I will fuel my dreams with this marvelous celebration of the whitetail deer, the greatest game animal in the world. God bless the whitetail deer, and long may his tribe continue to thrive!

Craig Boddington
PASO ROBLES, CALIFORNIA

How to Score Whitetail Deer

Jack Reneau, Wm. H. Nesbitt, and Philip L. Wright

CERTAIN COMMONALITIES EXIST IN THE MEASURING OF TROphies and are presented here as an introduction to the measuring process. Sportsmen should be aware of these general procedures as he or she begins the process of measuring a trophy animal. With a minor investment in equipment, almost anyone can make a reasonably accurate measurement of his or her big game trophies. In fact, it is likely that you already have some of the equipment needed to perform accurate measurements.

Without a doubt, the single most useful piece of measuring equipment is a 1/4-inch wide, flexible steel measuring tape, graduated in sixteenths of an inch. It can be used to take all length and circumference measurements required by the scoring system. Such tapes come equipped with either a "ring-end" or a "clip-end." The ring-end tape, equipped with a blank space before the zero mark, is the most useful since it can be used to take all circumference measurements, as well as all length measurements. With the ring-end tape, the circumferences can be read at the zero point; with a clip-end tape, you must read your measurements at some increment (e.g. 10-inch mark) greater than zero, and then subtract the increment to arrive at the correct measurement.

A round, flexible steel cable and an alligator clip can be used for taking point and main beam length measurements on antlered animals only in place of the 1/4-inch wide, flexible steel measuring tape.

MEASURING EQUIPMENT CHECK LIST

- ☐ 1/4-inch steel tape
- ☐ Flexible steel cable
- ☐ 2 carpenter's levels (with c-clamps)
- ☐ Folding carpenter's ruler
- ☐ Masking tape
- ☐ Pencil
- ☐ B&C score chart

The best way to mark a baseline is to use masking tape and a pencil. This will aid in getting proper and accurate length of point measurements and the tape can then be easily removed without marking on the antlers.

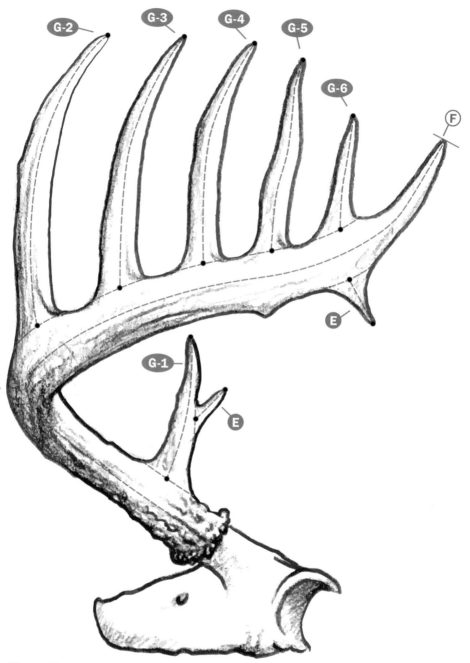

Figure A

The typical pattern of mature whitetail antler development is an unbranched main beam that normally develops from three to seven (or more), usually paired, unbranched points off the top of the main beam at spaced intervals. Point lengths are measured between black end points. **E = Abnormal Points**   **F = Main Beam**   **G = Points**

Another useful piece of equipment is a system for taking greatest spread measurements. A very accurate set up consists of two carpenter's levels with c-clamps affixed to one end to serve as bases so the levels are free-standing. The right angles formed by the upright levels (final positioning by the bubbles) form the boundaries for the measurement line, which is read with a steel tape or folding carpenter's rule.

A folding carpenter's rule with a brass slide is indispensable for taking inside spreads. As necessary, the rule is unfolded and the extension is used to accurately determine spread measurements.

Finally, but certainly not least, copies of the current copyrighted score charts are needed to perform accurate measurements. Current copyrighted score charts can be downloaded in PDF format from the Club's web site (www.boone-crockett.org).

SCORING WHITETAIL DEER

Whitetails can show an almost infinite variety in number and location of points. The non-typical category was established to properly recognize such trophies and there are typical and non-typical categories for both Coues' and whitetail trophies.

In the following material, the scoring procedure for whitetails will be described. Of course, the instructions apply equally well to Coues' deer, with the only difference being minimum entry scores. The typical pattern of mature whitetail antler development is an unbranched main beam that normally develops from three to seven (or more), usually paired, unbranched points off the top of the main beam at spaced intervals (Figure A). These are the normal points. Usually, a brow tine develops in this pattern as the first normal point, G-1, and the second normal point, G-2, on each side is usually the longest of the sequence. As in other deer categories, the main beam tip is counted as a point but is not measured as a point as it is part of the main beam measurement. All points that come off of normal points, abnormal points, burrs, bottoms and sides of the main beam are abnormal points. There are other abnormal points that will be discussed in more detail on the following pages.

Once you have identified the normal points, you need to decide if the deer should be scored as a typical or non-typical. In most cases it will be quite obvious. If there is any doubt, consider the number of abnormal points. If there are no or few abnormal points, the rack should obviously

FIGURE B

Establish a baseline that reflects the normal antler shape as if the point were not present. The point length is measured between the two black end points.

be scored as a typical. If there are numerous abnormal points, use the non-typical score chart. Regardless, there is no difference in how typical and non-typical whitetail deer are scored; all measurements are the same in both categories. The real difference between the two categories is that the total of the lengths of the abnormal points is deducted to arrive at the typical score and added in to arrive at the non-typical score.

Once you have scored a trophy, you can transfer the measurements from a typical score chart to a non-typical score chart to determine the non-typical score. If you used a non-typical score chart, you can transfer the measurements to a typical score chart to arrive at the typical score for the same trophy. In most cases, a trophy will make the minimum in only one category. If a trophy qualifies for both categories, it is the owner's option to choose which one the trophy will be listed in as it cannot appear in both. It is strongly suggested, however, that such a trophy be listed in the category where it ranks the highest.

A point in whitetail is any projection at least one inch long and longer than wide at some location at least one inch from the tip of the projection (Figure L). (Each projection should be measured to ascertain whether it is or is not a point.) Once it is determined that a projection is a point then its entire point length is measured from its tip down to its base. As shown in Figure B, point base lines are established where the point joins either the main beam or another point. The base should reflect the normal antler configuration as if the point were not present.

The length of beam and antler point length measurement may be taken by the use of the flexible steel cable or a 1/4-inch wide, flexible steel clip-end tape. The use of a round, flexible steel cable (such as a modified compound bow cable available from B&C or a bicycle brake cable) greatly speeds-up the measuring process while still yielding an accurate measurement. However, only the 1/4-inch wide steel tape can be used for circumference measurements.

In the past, deer with skull plates that had been fractured or shattered by a bullet, dropping, etc., were not acceptable for entry in B&C. However, it is now possible to enter such trophies, so long as the pieces can be perfectly pieced back together and the spread measurements taken. Skull plates that have been sawn in half still are not eligible for entry in B&C. Each damaged skull is considered on a case by case basis.

For measurement of length, the cable is positioned along the outer curve of the beam or point. The end of the measurement is marked by attaching an alligator clip to the cable at the proper spot. The cable is then removed and held in a straight line against a folding carpenter's rule to record the length measurement. The clip-end tape is often faster to use when antler points are

> **WHOSE RIGHT?**
>
> When recording your measurements on the B&C score chart be sure to put them in the correct columns. And by RIGHT ANTLER... we mean the deer's right antler, not the right side as you are looking at the antlers.

generally straight as the clip-end can easily be hooked on the end of the antler point and the tape stretched across the point's base line. When using a 1/4-inch wide tape on a curved point or antler beam, the measurer will need to mark locations and pivot the tape along the line of measurement. Be sure to align the tape at the appropriate length when pivoting the tape.

The measurement for determining the length of an antler main beam is illustrated on the score chart, being generally a line from the antler burr, above the eye, to the beam tip, maintained along the outer side of the beam (Figure A). It can be measured either from the tip to the burr or from the burr to the tip.

The measurement begins at the point where the center line along the outer side of the base intersects the burr. This point is above and slightly off center of the eye socket. To determine this starting point, view the antlers from the side lining up the far side with the near side. Find the middle of the burr as the antlers are viewed from this angle (i.e., the center of the burr on the outer side). It is neither at the lower front edge nor at the rear edge of the beam but rather at the outside center of the burr.

Once the starting location on the burr is noted, the length of the main beam measurement proceeds along the outer side of the beam towards the middle of the antler beam below the G-2 point as indicated in Figure A. From that location, it proceeds on out to the beam tip over the outer curve of the antler. In general, this line should stay near the middle of the beam on the outer side. It is sometimes helpful to first mark the base lines for the normal points as this may provide a visual reference for staying in the middle of the antler beam. The actual measurement is best taken by the use of the flexible steel cable or steel clip-end tape. The use of a tape necessitates marking the antler with a soft lead pencil and swinging the tape at these marks as necessary as the antler curves. Either way should result in the same measurement if the correct line is chosen.

Prior to making the actual measurement by either method, it is often helpful to hold the rack in a normal, upright position at arm's length. This will show whether or not the chosen line properly follows the outer curve of the main beam.

If the antler beam rolls inward, still stay near the middle of the beam even though the middle may now be on the top and not on the true outer side of the surface of the antler. If the beam hooks upward, still stay on the outer side of the antler near the middle (and not over the curve of the upper hook, which would place the measurement line along the bottom of the beam). If an abnormal point (or antler projection) is slightly in the line of measurement, simply find the shortest path around the point either above or below the projection and continue the measurement.

In rare instances, it may be necessary to use calipers to determine an accurate length of main beam measurement because of an obstructing point or growth. If this is the case, make tick marks immediately before and after the obstruction to mark the path of the main beam through it. Then, measure the distance from the burr to the obstruction with a cable, and use calipers to measure the distance through the obstruction. Finish by measuring the distance from the opposite side of the obstruction to the beam tip with a cable. Record all three measurements and add them together to arrive at the length of the main beam and record it on the score chart.

In the case of webbed antlers, special care must be taken when measuring beam lengths. You must first project the normal main beam as if there was no webbing. The length is then taken through the center of the

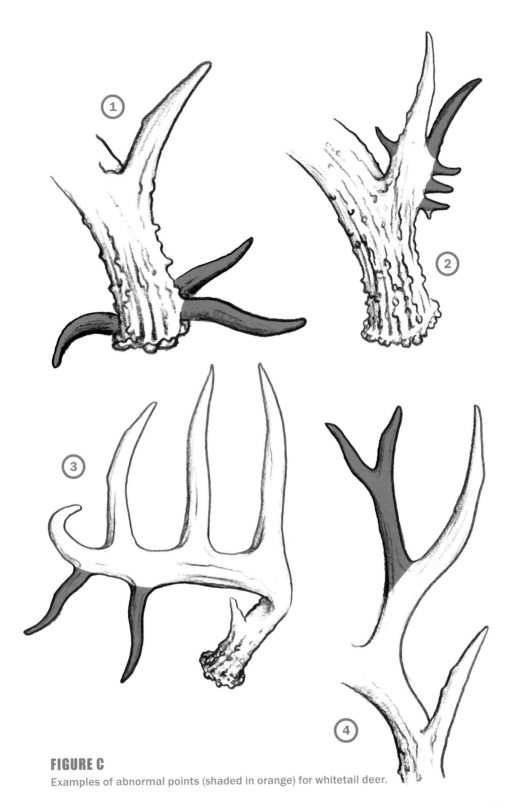

FIGURE C
Examples of abnormal points (shaded in orange) for whitetail deer.

projected main beam as usual. This measurement technique applies to any webbed antler, whether the webbing occurs on one or both antlers.

The next stage involves the measurement of point lengths (Figures C-1 through C-4). The designation of points as either normal or abnormal requires application of the following general rules:

1) Burr tines or "beauty points" (points arising from the antler burr) are always abnormal (Figure C-1).

2) Split or multiple brow tines mean that only one of these can be measured as the normal brow point. If one of these is a clear-cut branch of the other, the branch is designated as abnormal (Figure C-2). If both are separate points, without one being a branch of the other, choose as the normal G-1 point the one that best matches in shape and location usual G-1 points and the G-1 on the other antler. Generally this will be the longer point; the other(s) is then measured as abnormal.

3) Points arising from the side or bottom of the main beam are always abnormal (Figure C-3).

4) Point branches (those arising from points rather than the main beam) are always abnormal (Figure C-4).

5) Extra points occurring below the brow tine are always abnormal points even though they may be paired.

6) If two points (other than brow points) have a common base origin on the top of the main beam, and one is not a branch of the other, and both "pair" with points on the opposite antler, both are considered normal (Figure O).

7) Normal points arise from the top of the main beam at roughly spaced intervals and are usually paired with similar length points on the other antler in a more or less symmetrical pattern.

8) Paired points arising from the top of the beam are treated as normal points even though they may be shorter (or longer) than adjacent points and have slightly different spacing than other paired points. Thus, a pair of short points occurring between G-1 and the next set of taller points would be treated as G-2 points.

9) If a rack has two rows of side-by-side points on each antler, one row should be treated as abnormal points. Generally, the outer row points are measured as the normal points, and the inner row points off the top inside edge of the main beam are the abnormal points.

There are instances where a single point, usually paired with a similar

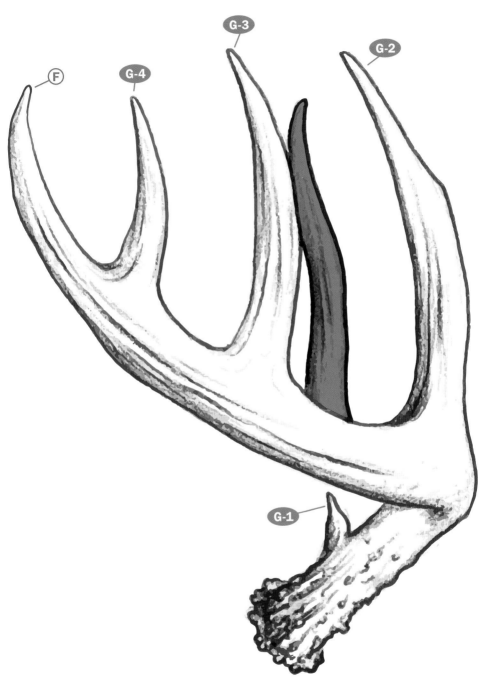

FIGURE D

There are instances where a single point comes off the top inside edge of the main beam not in line with the outer edge of the main beam and is considered an abnormal point (shaded orange).

The orange point is an unpaired normal point. Enter a dash or zero for the missing point on the other side.

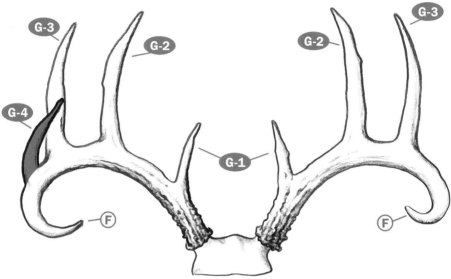

point on the opposite antler, comes off the top <u>inside</u> edge of the main beam (not in line with the outer edge of the main beam) and is considered an abnormal point. Such an offset point most commonly occurs between the normal G-2 and G-3 points (Figure D) and has two characteristics that identify it as abnormal. First, portions of the base overlap the base of another point on top of the main beam, causing the steel tape to twist or kink when taking a circumference measurement between such point and its neighbor. Second, and more obvious, is that such a point does not align with other normal points along the outside edge of the main beam and extends inward. If such an offset abnormal point (depicted in Figure D), occurs on only one antler, the matching point on the opposite side is also abnormal because it is a non-symmetry point.

10) Extra, unpaired points at the end of the beam that project upward and generally in the usual spacing pattern are treated as normal points (Figure E). Enter a zero for the missing point on the other side. Since these unmatched points at the end of the beam are "matched" against a zero value, their lengths will be subtracted in the difference column essentially negating their presence. The determination of these as normal points should be the same whether the trophy is entered in the typical or non-typical category.

11) If an "extra" point (unpaired, and not one of the normal pattern of points) arises from the top of the main beam and upsets the interval

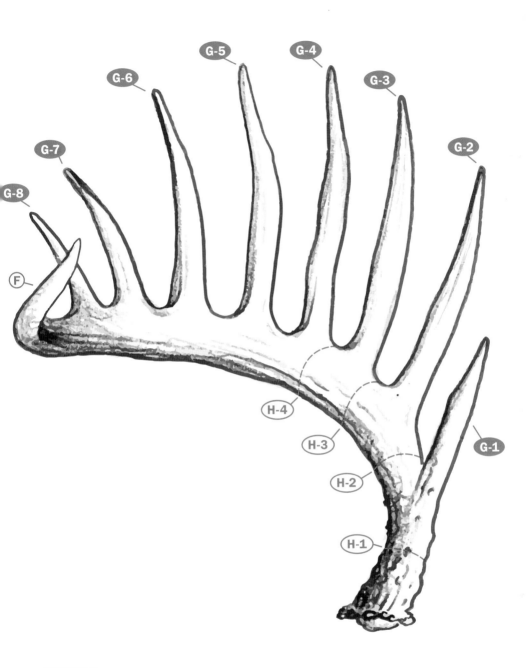

FIGURE F

There is no upper limit to how many normal points might occur on a whitetail trophy. Note locations of the circumference measurements.

Figure G

The most common unmatched point location is shaded in orange. That point is considered abnormal since it is not at the end.

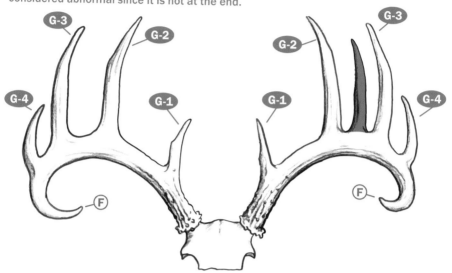

spacing/pairing (Figure G), it should be counted as abnormal (even though it is "normal" in origin) to avoid the artificial penalty for lack of symmetry between points that would occur if it were counted as a normal point. Such points are referred to as non-symmetry points and will be discussed in more detail in the material that follows.

12) There is no upper limit to how many normal points might occur on a whitetail trophy (Figure F), but the usual pattern is seven or fewer (plus beam tip) per antler, and the score chart reflects this pattern. In the extreme rarity that more than seven truly normal points occur, the measurements of the extra point(s) could be included as a separate additional line(s) on the score chart and explained in the REMARKS section.

13) If a G-1 point (brow tine) is missing on one antler, it is proper to treat the existing brow tine on the opposite antler as a normal point, and match it against a zero value for the missing G-1. There are actually three, and only three occasions, when an unmatched point off the top of the beam is treated as a normal point—a point opposite a missing brow tine that never grew (as described above), a point opposite a broken normal point less than an inch long, and an unmatched point at the end of the main beam.

The lengths of the individual normal and abnormal points are recorded in the proper blanks on the score chart. If a normal point has been broken off to less than an inch long, record a zero to indicate its condition and note the action in the REMARKS. Such action preserves the sequence and avoids any artificial penalty for non-symmetry.

Certain special cases—common base points, webbed points, burr points are covered later in this chapter. Additional comments are in order for the treatment of non-symmetry points. The rule is simple—if an extra unmatched point, that is a normal point by definition, occurs at some position other than at the end of the beam, it is treated as an abnormal point. Such points are referred to as non-symmetry points. If this point were paired on the opposite beam, it would be treated as a normal point. Thus a rack must display more normal points on one side than the other to even be considered as one that has a non-symmetry point. While these unmatched points can occur at any location, they are most common between G-2 and G-3 as illustrated in Figure G. One specific situation that may give rise to this situation is the presence of a common base point with G-2 on one side and a forked G-2 on the other. In such cases, it is likely the point sharing the common base with G-2 is extra as it may be "matched" against the fork, which is an abnormal point on the other side.

The key determination is which point is unmatched. If the point is unmatched at the end, then it is normal. If it is unmatched between normal points, it is abnormal. The determination is the same whether or not the deer is being measured as a typical or non-typical entry. In many cases, the decision will result in an overall lower score for the buck, particularly if it is being entered in the typical category. Such a result should occur since the measuring system for typical entries is designed to reward highly symmetrical, balanced antlers. An extra point detracts from this symmetry. Again, this ruling does not apply to an unmatched G-1 point, nor an unmatched point at the beam's end. In cases where a point is ruled a non-symmetry point, please use the REMARKS to highlight this decision.

Points are measured either from the base lines established on the main beam to the tip of each point or from point tip to the base line, with both methods yielding the same result. Generally, points end in a sharp cone shape, with the measurement being to the tip of this cone. Should the point end in a noticeably blunted condition, somewhat like a human thumb, the measurement line can be continued to the midpoint of the rounding. If a point (or beam) is broken and not a round blunt end, use a credit card or carpenter's square to "square off" the end in a fashion similar to the taking of the length of horn for sheep.

If a rack shows numerous points and/or many abnormal points, measurement of it can be aided by marking each point with bits of colored tape to designate normal points (perhaps green tape) and abnormal points (perhaps red tape). It is also very helpful to use a third color to indicate projections that do not qualify as points so that they are not inadvertently and incorrectly measured as points. As each point is measured to its proper base line, the tape is removed to show that the point has been measured. (Remember the beam tip is not measured as a point.)

Establishment of the base lines for individual point measurement is straightforward. The base line is established to identify that material properly called main beam from the material of the point (or separate a point branch from its "parent" point). Properly drawn, the base line should delineate the same amount of beam (or "parent") material below the point's center as can be ascertained on either side of the point being measured. A good method of marking base lines is to pull a measuring cable across the point base resting on top of the parent structure antler material.* Then the base line is marked with a lead pencil along the lower edge of the cable.

Antler points are then measured along the outside of their curve. In almost every case, the points G-2, G-3, G-4, and others in the sequence, curve inward and not outward. If a point should curve outward, it would be appropriate to measure it on the inside of the rack and thus reflect properly the outer curve of the point. In the case where it is not obvious which direction the point curves, measure both sides and record the longer measurement as the point length. It is never correct to measure along the edges of a point to determine its length. The same procedure of measuring points on the outside of their curve applies to abnormal points as well.

The brow tines, although usually straight, may be curved either backward or forward. If they are curved forward, they are measured on the backside in order to reflect the outer curve of the point. If they are curved backward, they are measured on the front side, again to reflect the outer curve. Note such actions in the REMARKS.

The four circumferences (H-1, H-2, H-3, and H-4) are taken by use of the ring-end measuring tape. The tape should be positioned in the general area of the indicated measurement by looping it around the main beam. Pull the tape together and gently slide it back and forth along the beam until the smallest circumference measurement is obtained. If you use a clip-end tape to measure circumferences, overlap the tape at a full 10

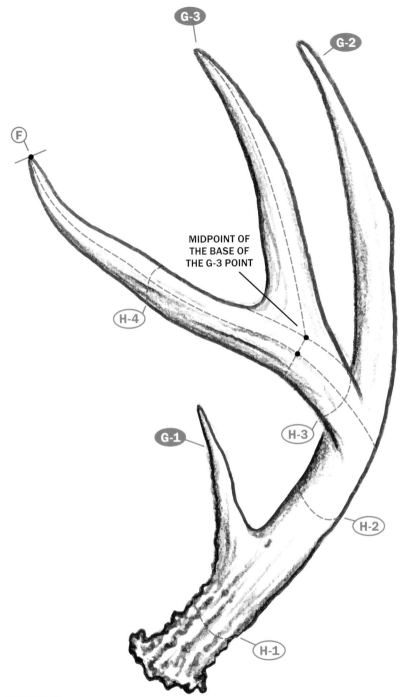

MIDPOINT OF THE BASE OF THE G-3 POINT

FIGURE H

Draw a line across the outside curve of the main beam (perpendicular to its length) from the midpoint of the base of the G-3 point. Then measure the distance from the perpendicular to beam tip. The location for H-4 is then determined by dividing that distance by 2.

inch increment to simplify the procedure. Be sure to subtract the amount of overlap before recording the measurement.

Almost without exception whitetail trophies large enough to reach the current All-time records book minimum entry score (170 for typical; 195 for non-typical) will have at least five normal points (including beam tip) on each antler. For such trophies, the four circumferences will be taken between points as illustrated on the score chart. In some cases, there may be only three measured points per antler, which will require that the H-4 circumference be taken halfway between the G-3 point and the antler tip (Figure H). To make this measurement properly, determine the center of the base of G-3 where it meets the main beam, then measure from this center point to the beam tip. The halfway point of this line is the correct location for the H-4 circumference.

The inside spread should be taken with a folding carpenter's rule, utilizing the extension to complete the measured line. Care must be exercised to properly position the ruler for this measurement. The line of measurement should be at a right angle to the long axis of the skull. It

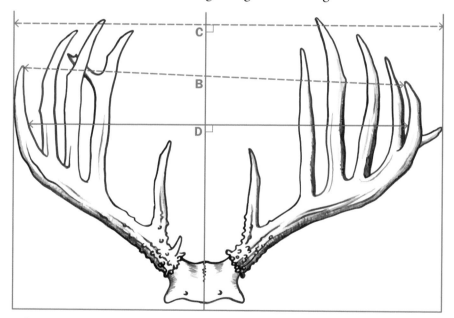

FIGURE I

Positioning for the three spread measurements, two (C and D) of which are taken at right angles as noted in the figure above. The tip-to-tip spread (B) and the greatest spread (C) are necessary, but do not add into the final score. The inside spread (D) is entered as the spread credit, but may not exceed the length of the longer main beam.

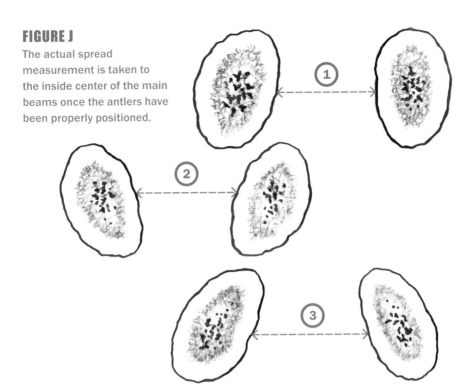

FIGURE J

The actual spread measurement is taken to the inside center of the main beams once the antlers have been properly positioned.

must also be parallel to the skull cap (Figure I). Thus, if one beam should be positioned higher than the other, it will be necessary to utilize a carpenter's square against the higher antler to properly locate the line. The actual measurement is taken to the center of the main beams once it has been properly positioned.

The actual measurement is taken to the inside center of the main beams once the antlers have been properly positioned. The correct points of contact for taking the inside spread measurement are noted in Figure J-1, which represents the cross sections of the main beams. If the main beams roll inwards or tilt outwards, the inside spread is taken to the centers of the main beams as illustrated in Figure J-2 and Figure J-3, respectively.

Note that spread credit cannot exceed the length of the longer antler main beam. If the spread measurement does exceed the longer main beam, enter the longer main beam length (rather than the inside spread measurement) in spread credit box of the score chart.

Rarely, one antler will curve inward in the normal fashion, while the other will flare outward. In such a case, the point of measurement for inside spread should not be taken on the flaring antler beyond where it begins to diverge from the "normal" curvature as found on the other antler.

The supplementary data of tip-to-tip spread should also be taken by use of the folding carpenter's rule or measuring tape. This measurement is simply from the center of the tip of one antler to the center of the tip of the other. Greatest spread is best taken by use of two perpendiculars, such as carpenter's levels held upright by large c-clamps or perfectly square-cut wooden blocks, that are positioned on each side of the rack. The measurement is then taken by a steel measuring tape or folding carpenter's rule between the perpendiculars.

ADDITIONAL SCORING TECHNIQUES: More on Point Measurements

Prior to January 1989, the definition of a point was open to more than one possible interpretation. The definition was then rewritten to clarify the approach and to have wording that is clearly stated and open to only a single interpretation. The definition of a point is as follows: To be counted a point, the projection must be at least one inch long, with the length exceeding width at one inch or more of length. Once it is established that a projection is a point, its length is then taken from the tip to the base line of the point. The only exception to this rule is for caribou for which the point must be at least one-half inch long and longer than wide at length one-half inch or more. Figure K provides illustrations of applications of this definition.

In some cases the length of a point may exceed 1" and the width of the base is greater than the overall length of the point. This may still be a point as long as the measurer can come down one inch or more from the tip and find a location where length exceeds the width at that location. Once it is determined that a projection qualifies as a point, it is measured from its tip to its naturally occurring baseline. Figure L illustrates this situation.

Several questions have arisen in the past concerning the determination of whether a projection was a point or not. Some measurers were taking the width of a point at an angle other than 90 degrees when ascertaining whether or not a projection was a qualifying point. This is an appropriate procedure when measuring along the point's natural base but not at other times. In 1998, the Records Committee approved the following clarification for point determination. Unless taken at the point's natural baseline, the width must be taken perpendicular to the length when determining whether or not a projection qualifies as a point. See Figure M.

When measuring a point or beam, or when taking a circumference,

FIGURE K

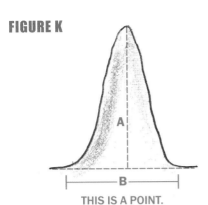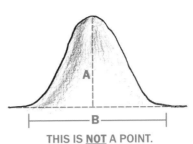

THIS IS A POINT.
A is longer than 1" and B is less than A.

THIS IS **NOT** A POINT.
A is longer than 1" and B is more than A.

FIGURE L

GH is greater than AD. Because AB is 1", and AC is longer than EF is wide, this is a point. Measure length AD.

FIGURE M

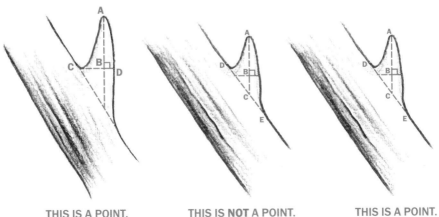

THIS IS A POINT.
AB = 1"
CD = 6/8"

THIS IS **NOT** A POINT.
AB = 1"
AC = 1-1/8"
DE = 1-2/8"

THIS IS A POINT.
AB = 1"
AC = 1-4/8"
DE = 1-2/8"

33

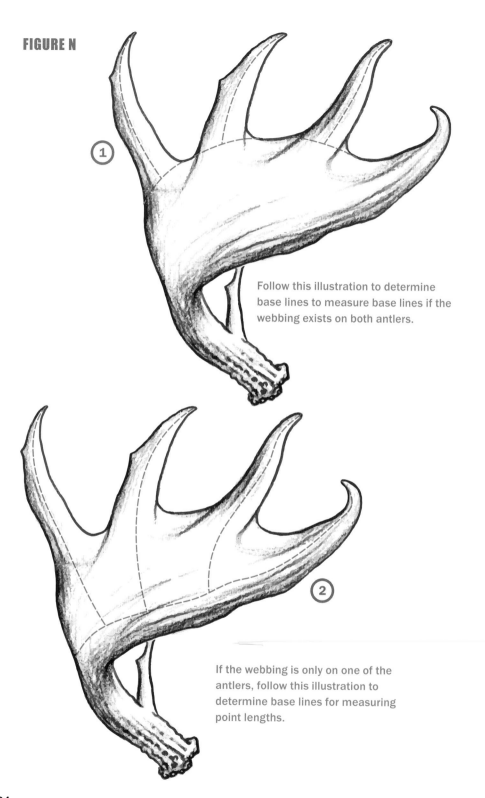

FIGURE N

① Follow this illustration to determine base lines to measure base lines if the webbing exists on both antlers.

② If the webbing is only on one of the antlers, follow this illustration to determine base lines for measuring point lengths.

the measurement does not always fall exactly on an eighth-inch mark. The measurer should round the value to the nearest eighth inch, and if the measurement falls exactly on a sixteenth-inch mark, the measurer should round to the next higher eighth-inch mark. In the case of skull measurements, the measurer rounds to the nearest sixteenth of an inch. If a measurement falls exactly between sixteenths, the measurement is again rounded up. One situation where the round-up rule does not apply is in the case of point length determination. Here the projection must be at least one-inch long. Thus a 31/32-inch long projection cannot be a point as it is not at least one inch long.

Occasionally, "palmation" or "webbing" may occur on one or both antlers so that there is a noticeable "filling-in" between individual points. If both antlers are palmated, establish the individual point base lines on the top edge of the palmation, then measure points and circumferences in the usual manner (Figure N-1). The trophy will receive credit for the symmetry of webbing on both antlers via the increased circumference measurements. If only one antler is palmated, draw the individual point base lines along the main beam where it would be if there was no palmation and then measure the individual points to this line (Figure N-2). In this case, the lack of symmetry caused by the webbing will be penalized by the circumference measurement differences, justifying the allowance for point length "hidden" in the webbing.

Common base points present certain issues that need to be addressed when measuring a trophy. Simply stated common base points are points that are joined at their bases and share some degree of webbing between them. Frequently, it is difficult to determine if two points are sharing a common base, or if one is a branch of the other. In order to be treated as common base points, and not as a point with an abnormal point branch, the cross section of the bases of both points must be a figure eight shape, as Figure O-1 demonstrates, if both points were cut off at their bases. This cross section must be clearly a figure eight. Two points (Figure P) with an oval-shaped base or with a base that is half oval and the remainder figure-eight shaped must be treated as a single point with an abnormal branch point. Both points are normal only if they are matched with normal points on the other antler and only if both points are lined up on the outside edge of the beam (Figure O-1).

Common base and webbed points differ. Webbing is the filling-in with antler material of two clearly separate points that are not joined together

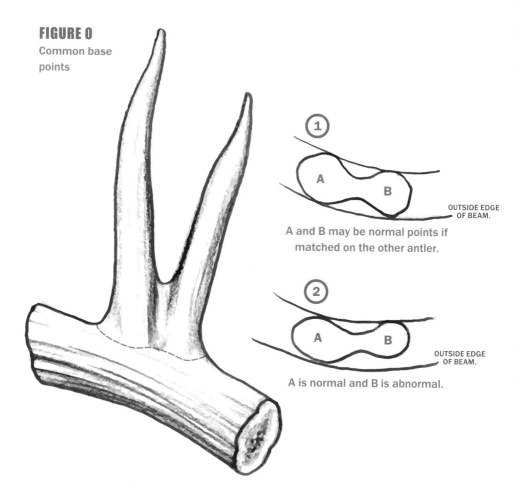

FIGURE O

Common base points

OUTSIDE EDGE OF BEAM.

A and B may be normal points if matched on the other antler.

OUTSIDE EDGE OF BEAM.

A is normal and B is abnormal.

except by the webbing. Common base points are two separate points joined together at the base that, as they merge together, share common point material. While they are not the same, the measuring technique is similar. If the common base points are found only on one antler, the point lengths are measured from their tips to the main beam (Figure Q-1). If the condition occurs at or before G-4 and involves normal points, the corresponding circumference measurement will be inflated. This increase is compensated for by the corresponding increase in the difference column associated with the measurement of the opposite side circumference.

If both sides of the antlers display common base normal points that occur at or prior to G-4, it would be inappropriate to measure both points to the beam and then to also record the inflated circumference measurement brought about by the shared point material. As both sides now display the shared webbing, no compensating deduction in the difference column

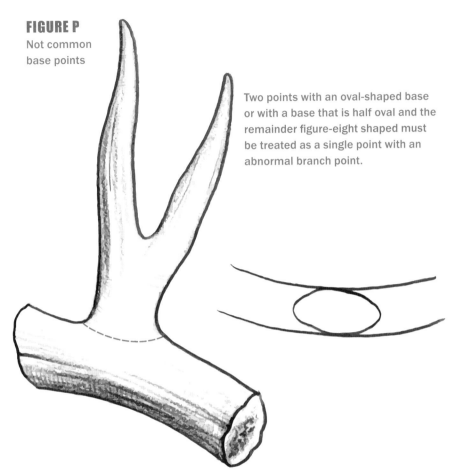

Two points with an oval-shaped base
or with a base that is half oval and the
remainder figure-eight shaped must
be treated as a single point with an
abnormal branch point.

would occur. Thus, if matched pair, common base points occur on both antlers, the base line for these points is established by moving it parallel to the main beam upwards through the lowest part of the gap between the common base points (Figure Q-2). The points are then measured from their tips to their centers on this adjusted base line.

Often the question of whether a point is one, two, or more points arises when a point that forks into several tips occurs. Such cases are most common on brow tines but also are present on abnormal point clusters. Some of these clustered points display common base type structures; others are simply a point with forks. The proper interpretation in such cases is that each projection, when measured from its tip to the bottom of the gap between them, must separately meet the definition of a point which is any projection at least one inch long and longer than wide at some location at least one inch from the tip of the projection is a point. Thus, for

FIGURE Q

①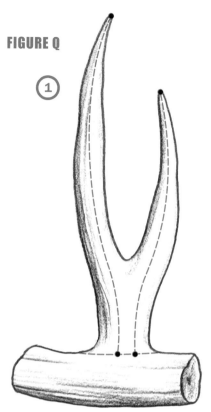

②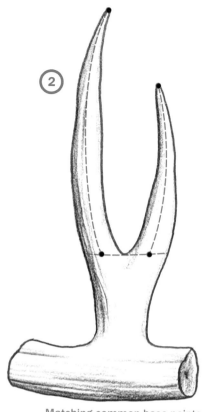

Common base points on **one side**. Measure point lengths between black end points.

Matching common base points on **both sides**. Measure point lengths between black end points.

FIGURE R

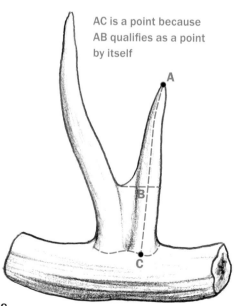

AC is a point because AB qualifies as a point by itself

A

B

C

FIGURE S

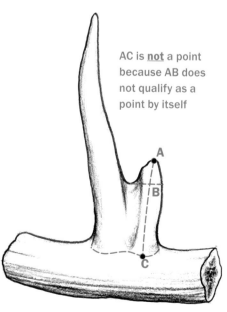

AC is **not** a point because AB does not qualify as a point by itself

A

B

C

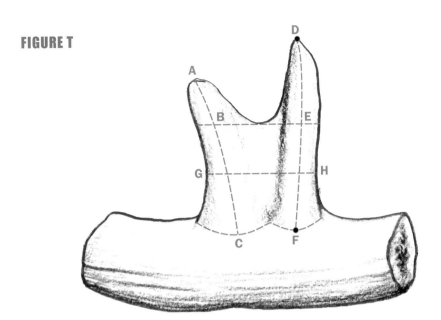

AB and DE are less than 1", hence, not two separate points. DF qualifies as a point since DH is longer than 1" and greater in length than GH width.

example, if a point that splits into two tips arose from the beam, each tip when measured from its tip down to the bottom of the gap between the tips must individually qualify as a point for this structure to be treated as having two separate points. Otherwise, it would simply be measured as one point. Figure R illustrates this procedure. While Figure J demonstrates the proper techniques to use when the projections in question share a common base, the same principle holds when one of the projections is a branch off the other. In Figure S, A-B and D-E are not two separate points themselves because neither projection qualifies as a point above the webbing. However, the whole structure could be classified as a single point only as long as it, measured from either tip to the base, qualifies as a point. This structure is then measured only from A-C or D-F, whichever is longer. Figure T illustrates a situation where the length of D-F is longer than AC.

Burr points are those points that develop directly as part of the burr material. In order for these projections to qualify as a point, the definition of a point is once again applied. A key step in determining whether or not a burr projection is a qualifying point is the establishment of the proper base line. Since the burr itself is part of the main beam, the measurer must treat the natural burr shape as beam and exclude it when establishing the

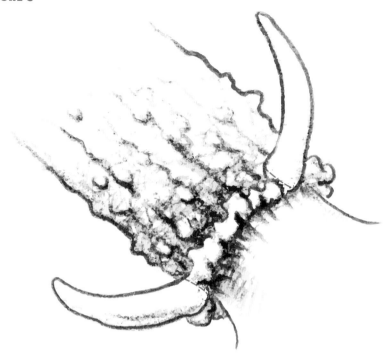

To determine the base lines on burr points, draw the line from burr edge to burr edge across the point, not to the inside edge of the burr.

base line. Figure U demonstrates the proper procedure for establishing a base line for a burr point. Essentially the line is drawn from burr edge to burr edge across the point, not to the inside edge of the burr. If the trophy is not mounted, the measurer can often find the base of the burr by looking on the underside of the burr to determine the end of burr material.

One other procedure to note concerns the measurement of abnormal points or crown points that project from the juncture of two points. These points are often joined in a web that reflects antler material not yet measured. If one simply draws a base line from edge to edge across the point, one is shorting the point some of its true length. Thus, the measurer should project the natural curve of the antler as if the webbing were not present for the base line for the length measurement in this situation. Figure V provides an illustration of this procedure. Often the measurer can determine a visual reference for this base line by comparing it to the other antler.

Official measurements cannot be taken until the antlers have air dried at normal room temperature for least 60 days after the animal was

FIGURE V

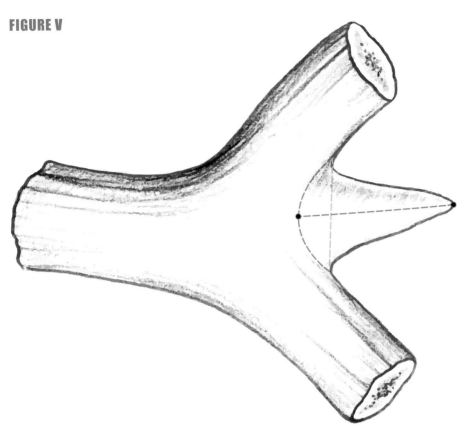

Project the natural curve of the antler as if the webbing were not present for the base line for the length measurement. The lighter orange base line is incorrect. Point length is measured between two black end points.

killed. If the trophy has been frozen prior to cleaning, as is often the case with skulls, the 60-day drying period begins once the cleaning process is complete. The drying process for trophies that have been boiled or freeze-dried starts the day they are removed from the boiling pot or freeze-drier, respectively.

In the case of picked up trophies, the 60-day drying period also applies. If it is clear from the condition of the antlers, horns, skulls, or tusks that the trophy has dried for more than 60 days, one does not have to wait another 60 days from when it was found to measure it. However, it is necessary to enter the approximate date the animal died on the line provided for the date of kill on the score chart. Trophy owners may be asked to provide a brief history for "picked up" trophies or trophies of unknown origin to substantiate the approximate date of death.

TYPICAL WHITETAIL SCORE CHART

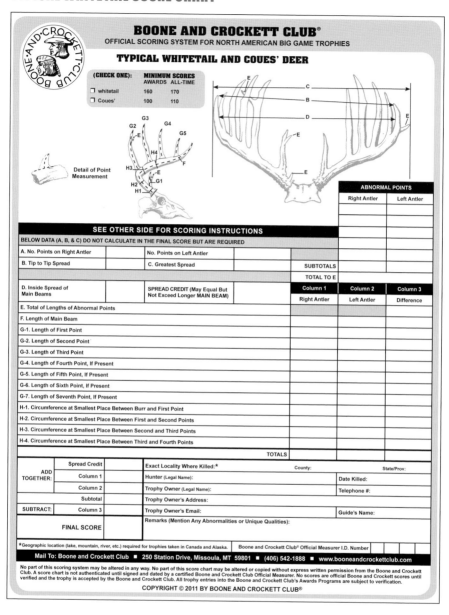

Official Boone and Crockett Club score charts can be downloaded free of charge from the Club's web site at www.boone-crockett.org. You can also order printed versions for a small fee directly from B&C by calling 406-542-1888.

NON-TYPICAL WHITETAIL SCORE CHART

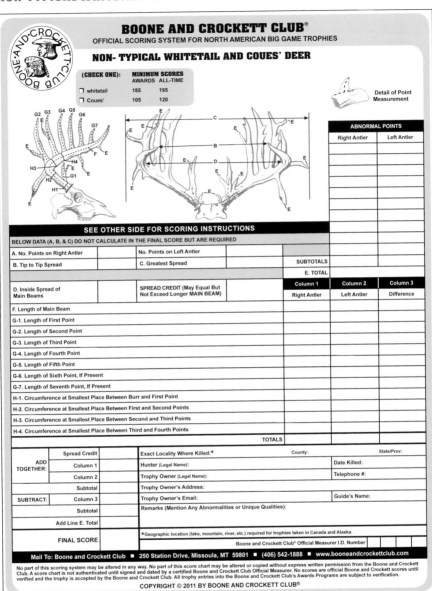

BOONE AND CROCKETT CLUB®

OFFICIAL SCORING SYSTEM FOR NORTH AMERICAN BIG GAME TROPHIES

NON- TYPICAL WHITETAIL AND COUES' DEER

(CHECK ONE):	MINIMUM SCORES	
	AWARDS	ALL-TIME
☐ whitetail	185	195
☐ Coues'	105	120

Detail of Point Measurement

ABNORMAL POINTS	
Right Antler	Left Antler

SEE OTHER SIDE FOR SCORING INSTRUCTIONS

BELOW DATA (A, B, & C) DO NOT CALCULATE IN THE FINAL SCORE BUT ARE REQUIRED

A. No. Points on Right Antler		No. Points on Left Antler				
B. Tip to Tip Spread		C. Greatest Spread			SUBTOTALS	
					E. TOTAL	

				Column 1	Column 2	Column 3
D. Inside Spread of Main Beams		SPREAD CREDIT (May Equal But Not Exceed Longer MAIN BEAM)		Right Antler	Left Antler	Difference
F. Length of Main Beam						
G-1. Length of First Point						
G-2. Length of Second Point						
G-3. Length of Third Point						
G-4. Length of Fourth Point						
G-5. Length of Fifth Point						
G-6. Length of Sixth Point, If Present						
G-7. Length of Seventh Point, If Present						
H-1. Circumference at Smallest Place Between Burr and First Point						
H-2. Circumference at Smallest Place Between First and Second Points						
H-3. Circumference at Smallest Place Between Second and Third Points						
H-4. Circumference at Smallest Place Between Third and Fourth Points						
			TOTALS			

ADD TOGETHER:	Spread Credit		Exact Locality Where Killed:*	County:		State/Prov:
	Column 1		Hunter (Legal Name):		Date Killed:	
	Column 2		Trophy Owner (Legal Name):		Telephone #:	
	Subtotal		Trophy Owner's Address:			
SUBTRACT:	Column 3		Trophy Owner's Email:		Guide's Name:	
	Subtotal		Remarks (Mention Any Abnormalities or Unique Qualities):			
	Add Line E. Total					
	FINAL SCORE		*Geographic location (lake, mountain, river, etc.) required for trophies taken in Canada and Alaska.			
			Boone and Crockett Club® Official Measurer I.D. Number			

Mail To: Boone and Crockett Club ■ 250 Station Drive, Missoula, MT 59801 ■ (406) 542-1888 ■ www.booneandcrockettclub.com

Field Judging Whitetail Deer

Jay Lesser | B&C Professional Member
Richard T. Hale | Chairman, B&C Big Game Records Committee

How to field judge for trophy quality is one of the most frequently asked question the Boone and Crockett Club headquarters receives. Knowing what a deer might score relative to the area you are hunting can be valuable information to have prior to committing to taking a shot. Whether for assisting in age evaluation, bettering a previously taken buck, managing a property, or hitting the minimum for the B&C records book, more and more hunters are looking to sharpen these skills.

While nothing will replace actual experience in the field, the following two theories have helpful tips and information to get you started. We've also provided a scientific breakdown of the weight each measurement carries when calculating the final score based on the measurements of more than 7,500 typical whitetail deer entered in B&C Records Program.

USING THE DEER RULERS
By Jay Lesser

The first thing you will notice about a large whitetail buck's rack is the overall height and width, followed by the number of points, and mass. When assessing a potential trophy's score, we need to look at the lengths of the main beams, lengths of the points, the inside spread of the main beams, and the mass or circumference of the main beams at four locations.

These things can be quickly evaluated in the field with a few simple calculations. To do this we need things of known sizes to visually compare the antlers to and in this case we will use the deer's ears, eyes, and nose.

Non typical points either need to be very few or many to score well in the Boone and Crockett system. Typical and non-typical whitetail deer are measured exactly the same. The difference in the score is that the total of the lengths of the abnormal points is **deducted** to arrive at the typical score and **added in** to arrive at the non-typical score. This buck obviously has a lot of things going on, which may be hard to judge in the field. For non-typicals, it may boil down to the unique factor, not the score.

THE RULERS
FOR AN AVERAGE BUCK

16 inches = Ears, tip-to-tip in alert position (**A**)
6 inches = Base to tip of the ear (**B**)
8 inches = Center of the eye to end of the nose (**C**)
4 inches = Circumference of the eye (**D**)

While this can be an inexact science considering the range of sizes from the smaller body bucks in Texas to the bulky giants of Canada, we are going to throw out the biggest and the smallest and take an average of the most common whitetails found in North America. The average buck, with his ears in an alert position, has an ear tip-to-tip spread of roughly 16 inches. His ears will measures six inches from the base to the tip. The circumference of his eye is four inches, and from the center of the eye to the end of his nose should measure about eight inches. These will be our "rulers" for antler size estimation. If you are hunting in an area that traditionally produces huge-bodied deer, or conversely, if you are hunting in area that has smaller deer, you will need to adjust your "rulers" accordingly.

Assuming you can get a frontal view, estimating a buck's inside spread should be easy. Is he outside of his ear tips? If so, by how much? For example, if his main beam appears to be half an ear or three inches outside the ear tip (A) on each side, then by adding 6 to 16 we find that he has a 22-inch spread.

Judging the length of the main beams is next. A general rule of thumb is to look for a buck whose main beams appear to extend forward as far as the tip of his nose. However, by using this criterion alone, a long-beamed buck might be passed over if you only have a side view and the buck has a wide spread and/or its antlers turn sharply in so that the main beam tips nearly touch. Also, be aware of the buck whose beams tower above its head before sweeping forward as this adds valuable inches to an otherwise average looking main beam. The actual main beam length is estimated using our ear length (B) and eye-to-nose rulers (C) illustrated on the facing page.

Next, and to many, the most impressive features of a trophy whitetail are the number and lengths of the points on his rack. The Boone and Crockett Club defines a point on a whitetail deer as "any projection at least one inch long and longer than it is wide at one inch or more of length." Since most whitetails are hunted in or near heavy cover where there may only be seconds to assess their antlers, we need a quick way to count points.

Points may be quickly counted by assuming that an overwhelming majority of mature whitetail bucks grow a brow tine on each antler and that the main beam tip usually lies almost horizontally. This allows us to count the standing normal points G-2, G-3, G-4, etc., and quickly add that to the number 2 (brow tine and beam tip). With this method you can quickly determine that a buck with two standing normal points per side is a 4x4 or

8-pointer, and with three standing points per side he is a 5x5 or 10-pointer, and so on. Nearly all the bucks that make the records book have at least five normal points per side. The length of the points can be estimated using the same "rulers" we used for the main beams.

The typical pattern of a mature whitetail's antler development is an unbranched main beam that normally develops from three to seven (sometimes more) unbranched points per antler at roughly spaced intervals. Any other points are considered "abnormal" and their lengths are deducted from the score if the buck is scored as a typical or added to the score if it is being scored as a non-typical.

Estimating the mass or circumference measurements of the antler is where we use our deer's four-inch eye circumference as the ruler (A). Compare the antler at H-1, H-2, etc., to the eye. How much bigger is the antler? If it were half again bigger, the circumference measurement at that point would be about six inches.

The main beam length is crucial to the score of a buck, accounting for roughly 30% of the score. A long-beamed buck might be passed over if you only have a side view and the buck has a wide spread and/or its antlers turn sharply in so that the main beam tips nearly touch. Also, be aware of the buck whose beams tower above its head before sweeping forward as this adds valuable inches to an otherwise average looking main beam.

A general rule of thumb is to look for a buck whose main beams appear to extend forward as far as the tip of his nose. It may appear at first glance that this buck's main beam length meets that criteria, but use caution, his head isn't in a full profile.

© istockphoto.com | JanelleStreed

CONTRIBUTING MEASUREMENTS

The pie chart below breaks down the weight each measurement gives to the final score of a whitetail buck. Data based on averages for over 7,500 records-book entries accepted in the Club's Records Program.

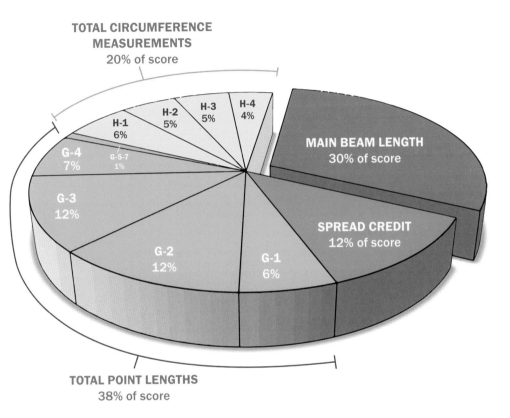

TOTAL CIRCUMFERENCE MEASUREMENTS
20% of score

MAIN BEAM LENGTH
30% of score

SPREAD CREDIT
12% of score

H-1 6%
H-2 5%
H-3 5%
H-4 4%
G-4 7%
G-5-7 1%
G-3 12%
G-2 12%
G-1 6%

TOTAL POINT LENGTHS
38% of score

Average Measurement	Typical Whitetail	% of Score
25.625	**Main Beam Length**	30%
19.75	**Spread Credit**	12%
5.5	**G-1:** First Point Length	6%
10.125	**G-2:** Second Point Length	12%
10.125	**G-3:** Third Point Length	12%
6.25	**G-4:** Fourth Point Length	7%
0.875	**G-5-7:** Fifth - Seventh Point (if 6th and 7th point present)	1%
4.875	**H-1:** Circumference at Smallest Place Between Burr and 1st Point	6%
4.375	**H-2:** Circumference at Smallest Place Between 1st and 2nd Point	5%
4.5	**H-3:** Circumference at Smallest Place Between 2nd and 3rd Point	5%
4.125	**H-4:** Circumference at Smallest Place Between 3rd and 4th Point	4%

Ideally, the rack should be viewed from the front and the side especially when judging the main beams. However, this isn't always possible and sometimes you will just have to go with your gut feeling. But beware of the rear view, as it can be deceiving. From this angle you get an exaggerated impression of the antler's height and spread.

The most practical way to practice your field-judging skills is to estimate the score of mounted heads. Use the buck's "rulers" to estimate the score, then check your calculations by actually measuring the rack. With a little practice, you will be surprised how close your estimates will become. One last word of advice, when the time comes to shoot, don't bother looking at the antlers one more time. It can cause your nervous system to do strange things.

AN ALTERNATIVE LOOK AT FIELD JUDGING WHITETAIL DEER
By Richard T. Hale

The process of field judging whitetail deer has about as many methods as practitioners—most of which undoubtedly have merits and shortcomings. My personal process has been streamlined over the years as I have tried to simplify it, speed it up, and focus on the antlers as much as possible. I am not critical of other methods, which work well for some, no doubt. My process, described below, helps me get a quick, reliable estimate on a buck in the field. To utilize this technique properly, a hunter would need to have some experience looking at large-antlered bucks—hopefully putting a tape on a few as well. This is the shortcoming of my method. The advantage is that it works quickly, which really makes a difference.

I realize the opportunity to see, let alone harvest a Boone and Crockett buck is less than a once-in-a-lifetime experience for most hunters. I am also aware that most hunters are not going to pass up harvesting a mature buck just because it does not score enough to meet Boone and Crockett minimums. Most encounters with wild, free-ranging mature bucks are far from ideal for judging antlers. The following are a few lessons I have learned over 44 years of hunting, guiding and occasionally killing a trophy-class deer.

Because the window of opportunity for viewing a buck is often limited by daylight, cover, or movement, the more quickly we can glean the required data the more accurately we can make estimates. This is more important when viewing several mature bucks at once. For this and other reasons, I prefer to focus on antlers rather than unrelated anatomical features. Commonly used yardsticks like ears and skull length often vary in size as much as 15 percent, thus unnecessarily complicating the process.

A quick breakdown of the components that comprise the score are roughly as follows.

- Points: 40 percent
- Beams: 30 percent
- Mass: 20 percent
- Spread: 10 percent

A cursory glance at the numbers reveals several factors that will help focus our efforts for a quick and dependable estimate. Looking at the spread first, it is apparent that it is a small component of the score. Spread also is not as subject to variation as some other components. If you examine a copy of any Boone and Crockett records book, you will note the average inside spread of main beams for a 170-class typical deer will be very near 18 inches. Disregarding the freakishly wide and narrow entries, a high percentage will fall between 16 and 20 inches. If the deer you are looking at falls outside these averages, it is apparent at a glance, and a small correction can be factored into the score.

FAST FACTS: SPREAD
Spread is 10 percent of score and a normal variation is plus or minus two points. Time to estimate spread: 10 seconds.

Mass is approximately 20 percent of the score of a record-class buck. Again, other than freakish examples, a very high percentage will fall between 35 and 40 inches for the combined side-to-side total. At a glance, most can be simply classified as light, normal or heavy, with the small corresponding allowances made. I will call normal 18 inches per side. Thick, massive points which give the antlers so much character simply have no effect on the score. Unilateral webbing cancels out and will also have no effect.

FAST FACTS: MASS
Mass is 20 percent of score. Normal variation is plus or minus 2 points total, combined, both sides. Time to evaluate mass: 15 seconds.

It is apparent that spread and mass are not time-consuming to evaluate, nor generally subject to a high degree of variation. Both features can be reasonably appraised with a glance. If misjudged slightly, these two figures will not affect the estimate to any appreciable degree.

Let's move on to evaluation of beams. The average beam length for a trophy-class buck will average 25 inches. Beams that are shorter than 25 inches will have some telltale traits. Most common are the ones that stop short of the nose and point forward. It takes a very wide spread to get 25 or more inches from a beam with that configuration. Beams that come off the skull directed outward will often be short as well. Great beams show well. They come high off the head, rise up several inches, and begin to turn outward. If the spread exceeds 20 inches and/or they turn well inward or even cross at the tips, you are looking at long beams. Continuing past the tip of the nose they often turn upward on the ends. A beam that has all of these features will sometimes approach or even exceed 30 inches. If it does so on both sides, that is a 5 to 8 percent increase in score and needs to be calculated into any estimate.

FAST FACTS: BEAMS

Beams comprise 30 percent of the score and are subject to a wide range of variation. Beams that twist, curve and turn are relatively longer than they appear. Estimated time to evaluate beams: 30 seconds.

We have now spent approximately one minute to evaluate 60 percent of the score. Please pardon my focus on time, but it seems there is seldom enough time or light to see all I would like—more so when viewing a group of bucks at dawn or dusk!

Now we come to the points. This is the largest and most variable component of the score. It is also the most affected by asymmetry. The first thing to determine is number of typical-appearing points. It does not take long. If a buck has three points rising off the top of the main beam, it will be a 10-point score. Four points rising up will count as 12 points. Beware of upturned beams that appear to be points. They increase beam length and really improve the appearance of the rack but are not scored as a point.

Very few deer will make the B&C All-time minimum score of 170 as 8 points. This 8-point buck has long beams but the rack dwarfed the 240-pound body. He was short of the 170 minimum.

As with all features, it is important to count both sides whenever the view is possible.

Very few typical deer will score in the All-time records book as 8 points, and even fewer will have more than 12. We need to focus our efforts on the 10- and 12-point deer. Any 4x4 buck that scores 170 points will appear so large that few, if any, hunters would consider passing them. I have personally seen only one 4x4 buck alive that was over 170 points, and it was obvious. He was with another great buck and the choice was left to the

hunter. I am certain he is happy with his large non-typical buck, but more than 20 years later, I still think of the one he passed. All but the greatest of 8-points seem to fall a bit short, and they are easy to overestimate. I have only seen one buck with a 7-point typical side and the other side was shed off. Out of a couple thousand shed antlers I have picked up, only one that I recall had even a hint of a G-6.

Back to point evaluation: Once it is determined that the buck you are viewing is mature with 5 or 6 typical points per side, the more tedious part begins. Let's start with the brows. They and the G-4s are the most common areas of weakness of an otherwise high-scoring buck. Brows should be 5 or more inches on both sides and can vary a great deal—from missing one or both to being 12 inches long. I try to look at them first as they are more difficult to see in fading light, which is so often a factor. Next I view the G-4s. They should be a minimum of 6 inches. G-5s are always just icing on the cake.

Moving to the make or break area, look at the G-2s and G-3s. We need a total of 22 to 24 inches per side for the pair. Points of this length simply look long. If the G-2 starts lower on the beam and rises to the same level as the G-3, it will be approximately 2 inches longer. Good numbers in this area for an average 170-point deer are 12 and 11.

FAST FACTS.

Points are 40 percent of score. They are more time-consuming to evaluate and are subject to high variation in number, total length and symmetry. Points take far more time to evaluate than all other factors combined. We need to see 5 or 6 typical points per side with a cumulative total of 32 or more inches.

Time to evaluate varies; 60 seconds is about the minimum with usable light and a favorable angle for viewing.

Now that we have the basics down, there is the matter of putting it all together and arriving at an estimated score. Doing so requires consideration of two other factors: symmetry and non-typical points. Symmetry is easily calculated by simply figuring the short side. For example, if brows appear to be 5 inches and 8 inches, use 5. If the G-4s appear to be 6 inches and 9 inches, use 6 inches for both sides—really adds no time at all.

Non-typical points either need to be very few or many to score well in the Boone and Crockett system. Having many, of course, will place the

Some of the most common non-typical points are split G-2s such as the ones this B&C records-book buck demonstrates above. With a final score of 185-2/8 points, it just makes the minimum score for the non-typical category. It was arrowed by Jonathon M. Faulks in Wisconsin's Waupaca County in 2012.

deer in the non-typical category. The most common non-typical points are split brows, basal points and split G-2s. Basil points are often very difficult to see. It simply takes a bit of luck in that area. The older a buck is, the more likely he will have basil points as well as more non-typical points of all types. There is a reason that so many of the great typical deer are 4 years old. At that age, they can remain fairly free from extra non-typical points, while being old enough to express a large portion of their genetic potential for antler growth.

In general, a 170-point deer will need to have enough size to account for 4 to 8 inches of deductions including all non-typical points and deductions for non-symmetry. Some have much more, and a few have a very small amount. That means we need 78 or more typical inches of antler per side prior to deductions in most cases.

Non-typical points need to be very few or very many to score well with the B&C scoring system. Texas hunter AJ Downs harvested this 256+ non-typical in 2012. It has 19 non-typical points adding 124 points to the final score.

APPLYING THIS TECHNIQUE IN THE FIELD

Let's go through the process with a small bachelor group of bucks, just out of velvet. We will just be scouting, prior to season. At that time it is easier to focus on scoring. We will need to make a few assumptions to allow this to happen. We will say there are five mature bucks and we have five minutes of viewing light left. The exact time left is known as it has been noted every evening prior to this while scouting. No other deer are present, and all are unaware we have approached the bean field.

First look at body size and body language. When the deer are not alerted, the heads will be down about 70 percent of the time, feeding. Is one buck noticeably bigger, taller, more blocky? Is one hanging back closer to timber? Do the others give one a wider berth or avoid facing it directly? Is there another buck back inside the woods waiting for darkness? If any of these questions are answered yes, look that one over first. In this case we will decide all deer have similar merit and are in the field.

Time used: 30 seconds.

Next, wait for heads to rise. First one to raise its head is a 4x5—two up on one side, three on the other. No offsetting factors to increase score. Beams appear to stop at nose, point straight forward 22 inches. No non-typical points. G-2s and G-3s appear to be 10 inches each. Brows are 6 inches each, but the lone G-4 is only 4 inches. Mass is slightly lighter than normal. Spread is 16-1/2 inches. Deer appears to be 3 years old, average size, and in good general health. This deer, while mature, is simply not going to score well. Estimated quick score is 145.

Time used: 30 seconds.

Two more deer have their heads up. Both are 3-year-old 4x4s. Neither is as large as the first one. Examine tree lines to see if others are showing up. No more deer appear.

Time used: 10 seconds.

The fourth deer raises its head to look around, view the other bucks and make sure all is well. In doing so, the head is turned from one side to the other, slowly—perfect viewing opportunity. First thing that is apparent are four points rising from the top of either beam. Beams rise well off the head and turn in a bit at the tips. Good, not overly long, 25 inches. Spread is slightly above average, 19 inches. Mass is good, but not notably heavy, 18 inches. A strip of velvet hangs down from left beam, but no non-typical points are apparent. This deer has potential. It is time to look over the points.

Brows appear short, 3 inches each. G-2s rise off the top of the beam and are slightly shorter than G-3s; figure 9 inches on the G-2s and 11inches for the G-3s—good, but not exceptional. The G-4s and G-5s drop so far below the height of the previous points that they appear odd, almost stair-stepped. Estimate 4 inches and 2 inches. Age appears to be 4. This deer is a very good buck but not a 170-point deer. When even a small amount of asymmetry is accounted for, he simply will not score over 158-161 points—really an eye-catcher though, so note where he is for next year. A deer like this can really blow up. I have seen deer gain over 40 inches in one year.

Time spent: 2 minutes. (Too long.) Wider than average—12 points—often get too much time.

This whitetail, captured by the author on video, is a mature buck with great antler development. However, the short brow or G-1s will likely make him just shy of a records-book deer.

One minute 50 seconds viewing light remaining, according to the watch that hangs from the binocular strap.

The last buck has been facing away, mostly feeding, but occasionally raising his head. We have watched him in our peripheral vision but viewing opportunities have been limited. Shadows are darkening, the sun long set. The first thing that becomes apparent is that the beams project beyond the width of the deer's body by a couple of inches on either side, indicating an inside spread of 23 to 25 inches. Exceptional. Mass appears very slightly light at the base but carries it out well, 17inches per side.

As the buck turns and moves further into the field, the right side comes into view. Beams extend beyond nose, turn slightly upward but do not turn inward much. With the spread and rise off the head, they will measure 27 inches or a bit more. Again, well over the 25-inch norm. G-2s originate from the beam where they are still rising. On top, the tip of the left side is even with the tip of the left G-3. On the right, the point is shorter by 3 inches and split with a 4-inch fork. The G-3s appear to be near 11 inches, but as the deer turns, we notice an inward curve. Add an inch, making it 12. The G-2s are curved to match, which will make them 13 and 10 inches. The G-4s are 4 inches on the right and 7 inches on the left. (We will use the small side.) Other points appear well-matched, and no abnormal points are visible.

Brows are hard to see. Light is now poor. With a turn of the head, brow tines do not appear to be split but are no more than 4 inches each. Short. Now it is too dark to gain further information. The deer have remained unaware of our viewing. Time to quietly leave.

Due to rapidly failing light, no math was done on the last buck. As we walk along, the process begins.

- Spread 24-plus.
- Mass appeared slightly light but was carried out to the H-4 area; 17 inches per side
- Beams 27-plus, appear matched.
- Brows short, matched; 4 inches
- G-2, 10 and 13 inches; short side to 10
- G-3, 12 inches, matched
- G-4, 4 and 7 inches; short side to 4 inches
- Non-typical points, split right G-2; 4 inches
- No basil points apparent. Near impossible to tell in failing light.

Minimum Whitetail Deer Scoring 160 points

KEY STATISTICS

This typical whitetail deer exhibits several key factors for making the records book. It is a 5x5 buck with 10-2/8 inches of deductions.

- Spread Credit = 21-1/8 inches (A) | Record Book Average = 19-6/8 inches
- Main Beam Length = 27 inches (B) | Record Book Average = 25-5/8 inches
- Average Point Length = 7-5/8 inches | Record Book Average = 6-3/8 inches

Doing the math, we arrive at the following approximate score:

- Beams: 27
- Mass: 17
- Points: 4+10+12+4
- Total=74
- Doubled=148
- Spread=24
- Total=172 points

Subtracting 4 inches for the non-typical point of the right G-2 leaves 168 points for a final estimated score.

With the above numbers configured, it becomes apparent that none of the five bucks will make the All-time Boone and Crockett records book. It takes literally hundreds of mature bucks in a great area to find one that will score 170 points. Many great deer simply are not conformed to score well. Most do not live long enough to exhibit their genetic potential. If they do live long enough, the antlers often grow too many non-typical points to score well as a typical. This is due to age, injuries and possibly stress. These factors increase the incidence of abnormal points. That is what makes a true records-book typical buck too hard to find.

Walking back to the truck, we have time to think over what we have done to make this work. A most important part of any scouting trip is to have a plan in place so that we are mentally prepared to gather the data in a systematic manner. Failure to do so will result in simply knowing where some mature bucks live. That is nice to know, but it will not help much when trying to choose the best one. We fully evaluated five bucks within five minutes of locating them. Getting into position went well. That is where it all starts. Wind held or anticipated changes were properly allowed for. We remained unseen, stayed off the main deer access trails, and did not bump any deer.

We now know where there are several mature bucks to keep an eye on for next year. A determined hunter living in good deer country will take hundreds of such walks for each records-book buck that he locates. I enjoy the process and hope you do as well.

Maximum Whitetail Deer
Scoring 213-5/8 points

KEY STATISTICS

The World's Record typical whitetail deer is above average on all fronts as expected. It's a symmetrical 6x6 buck with only 7-1/8 deductions.

- Spread Credit = 27-2/8 inches (A) | **Record Book Average = 19-6/8 inches**
- Main Beam Length = 28-4/8 inches (B) | **Record Book Average = 25-5/8 inches**
- Average Point Length = 10-6/8 inches | **Record Book Average = 6-3/8 inches**

The Perfect Shot
Craig T. Boddington | B&C Professional Member

UNLIKE MANY TYPES OF GAME, MOST WHITETAILS ARE REL-atively habitual, so to some extent you can control your shot through your hunting technique, and you can choose exactly where you set up. Even in the more open West, savvy bowhunters achieve considerable success by stand-hunting along movement corridors between bedding grounds and feeding covers.

In the East, literally millions of American hunters are obligated by law to use shotguns and/or muzzleloaders. Fully rifled slug guns and some muzzleloaders have enough accuracy to cleanly take deer at 200 yards, but for most of those hunters, the practical range limit is around 100 yards. This is a handicap, but not so severe that it prevents hundreds of thousands of hunters from harvesting deer every year. With such range limitations, it doesn't make sense to set up over a feeding field. You can take a stand in heavy cover, where trails suggest deer are moving between feeding and bedding grounds. Or, in heavy or mixed cover, you can use calls or rattling antlers to lure deer to the gun. In many areas, deer drives—whether from human or canine drivers—are the traditional technique, and buckshot-loaded shotguns are often the arm of choice. Whether by choice or by law, if you limit your range with a bow, shotgun, or muzzleloader (or, for that matter, a handgun), you simply need to choose ground and technique that are likely to yield a shot you can handle.

Rifle-toting hunters have far more options, and indeed a shot at a whitetail deer can take almost any form, from very close to very far. This spread occurs almost everywhere whitetails are hunted. I think my closest shot at a whitetail came while I was sitting on a tree stand

I had back-to-back successful Canadian whitetail hunts in 2000 and 2001—but I earned it. I had made several trips without getting a chance at a mature buck. When the shot presented itself, I made sure my placement was spot on.

in South Carolina. Off to my left were heavy woods with an active scrape line along the edge. Directly in front of me a rectangular food plot stretched for around 250 yards, so of course I was expecting a shot somewhere on its farthest edges. At dawn a few does drifted past, and then nothing. It was late morning and it was getting hot, so I figured the chances of anything happening were approaching zero. I started blowing a grunt call every 20 minutes or so, just to pass the time.

I'm not sure whether I heard something or saw movement, maybe both, but after the second series, I froze and swiveled my eyeballs to leafy cover at the near end of the tree line. After a few seconds, a nice 8 pointer stepped out. I slowly raised my .30-06 and shot it at less than 10 yards.

Close encounters are most likely to occur from a stand or while rattling or calling, but they can occur almost anywhere. Longer shots are also possible almost anywhere. The Deep South is famous for its huge soybean fields that draw deer like magnets. It's this kind of hunting that gave South Carolina gunmaker Kenny Jarrett the name for his famous Beanfield Rifle—slightly heavy, flat-shooting, super-accurate, and designed to reach out across those southern bean fields. It could well have been a cornfield rifle, because wherever grain is grown, whitetail bucks are just as likely to be standing on the far side as on the near side.

And one mustn't forget the power line rights-of-way and logging roads that offer opportunities for longer shots even in the midst of heavy cover. One day in Georgia I was sitting in a tree stand overlooking a wide power line right-of-way with heavy conifers to my rear and on the far side. During a break in a heavy downpour, a buck stepped into the cut line to my right, and I shot it at about 40 yards. A day later, I shot another buck from the same stand—but this deer was slipping along the trees on the far side, and the shot was a bit over 200 yards.

Very few whitetail habitats in the country are as thick as the famous brush country of South Texas. It is in this region that hunters developed the technique of calling rutting bucks by horn rattling, which simulates a fight between two bucks. If you're rattling antlers

The heart and a good deal of the whitetail's lungs are well protected by shoulder bone in a shot like this one. Also the margin of error either left or right is small at this angle. This is not a shot to take offhand or from a wobbly position.

Photo courtesy of Len Rue Jr. | Reprinted with permission of Safari Press from The Perfect Shot, North America.

My preference is the central lung shot, which offers the greatest margin for error. Note that any decently constructed bullet in .25 caliber and up will kill a deer with proper shot placement.

Photo courtesy of Len Rue Jr. | Reprinted with permission of Safari Press from The Perfect Shot, North America.

along the edges of the thick stuff, you may get a very close shot. But this country is crisscrossed by a grid of cut lines, known as the famous senderos of South Texas, and it is always possible for a huge buck to walk under your stand—though you're much more likely to get a shot a couple hundred yards up the sendero.

It's almost impossible to categorize shots at whitetails. Several million whitetails are harvested annually, and it's probably fair to say the average shot is well under 100 yards. This is skewed by the fact that our greatest numbers of whitetails are found in the thick cover of the Deep South, the Northeast, and the upper Midwest. It's also skewed by those millions of hunters who use short-range equipment. In the West, shooting opportunities average a good deal longer, depending on how you hunt.

Wait till the deer stops, or lead the point of aim slightly. The heart, shoulder, and lung shots are marked with orange dots.

Photo courtesy of Len Rue Jr. | Reprinted with permission of Safari Press from The Perfect Shot, North America.

For several seasons, just for fun, I helped a buddy—an outfitter—guide hunters in the badlands and river-bottom country of eastern Colorado. During archery and blackpowder seasons, we mostly used deer stands set along the watercourses and overlooking natural funnels. It is difficult to get within bow range of plains deer, but it wasn't a great trick to set up shots within 100 yards, ideal for muzzleloaders.

During rifle season we still used some stands, which increased vistas, but we hunted much more by spot-and-stalk tactics. Even though the country is wide open and there is always the possibility for longer shots, most deer are taken within 200 yards. Another factor is that really big whitetails are just plain hard to come by. Big, fully mature bucks aren't exactly uncommon in all areas, but a buck that has survived several hunting seasons becomes so elusive, and often, so nocturnal that it is almost impossible to kill. I would never advocate taking any shot that you aren't absolutely certain you can make. But there is no telling when or where a big buck might present itself, and your chances of bagging it are much improved if you can handle the full range of potential opportunities, from very close to very far.

TAKING THE SHOT

Whitetail deer are amazing creatures. They have adapted to life in proximity with man, yet they have also adapted to the full range of harsh conditions, from the arid mountains of the Southwest to the bitter winters of northern Canada. All along the Rocky Mountain Front, somewhat to our dismay, they are proving themselves capable of competing with mule deer! Pound for pound, I rate the whitetail as a fairly tough creature. Hit poorly, it is able to take a great deal of punishment, and it can cover a surprising amount of ground even if hit fairly well. This is a bit of a problem. Even fatally hit game can be hard to follow up and recover in the close cover that whitetails commonly call home—and many whitetails are hunted on relatively small properties, where recovering even a well-hit buck that gets across the fence can be fraught with difficulties.

Of course, the whole purpose of this chapter is to avoid these difficulties—to make the perfect shot that precludes a lengthy follow-up. Unless the range is very close and you have absolute confidence in your ability to place the shot, I don't like the brain, neck, or spine shots. They are immediately fatal, or at least totally disabling, if executed correctly—but there is just too much margin for error. My preference is the central lung shot. From a broadside presentation, divide the body horizontally into thirds: top, middle and bottom. For a perfect lung shot, follow the back line of the rear leg up and shoot into the bottom half of the middle third. From various angles away from the broadside

This illustrates a quarting-on shot. Note how the shoulder bones obstruct much of the heart/lung area.

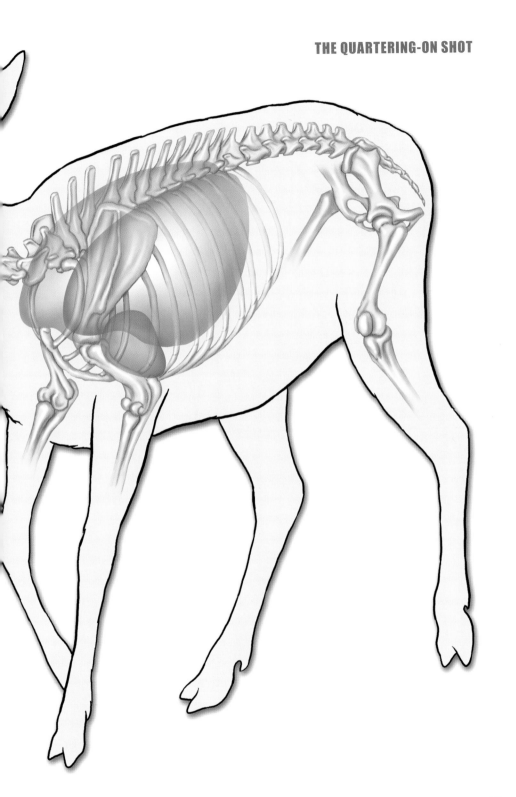

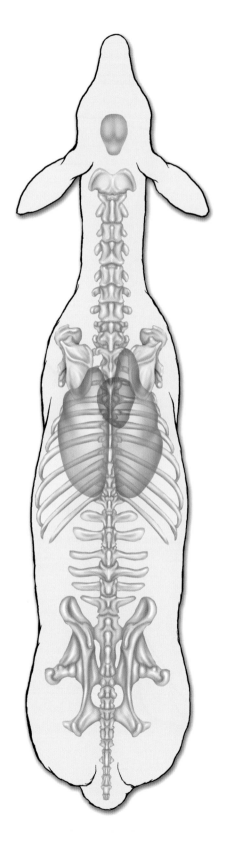

you must visualize where this area lies, but the good news is that, of all the surely fatal shots, the lung shot offers the greatest margin for error.

Whether the lung shot is immediately fatal depends a bit on luck. If the animal has just exhaled and is depleted of oxygen, a lung shot may well drop it in its tracks. If it has just inhaled, you may see very little initial reaction, but it should go down within 60 yards. The lung shot also offers the advantage of ruining less edible meat than the heart shot, but the heart shot is also a very good option.

The problem with a true heart shot is that it's a bit tricky, and you must consciously shoot a bit lower than most people wish to. From a broadside presentation, again divide the body horizontally into thirds. Follow the centerline of the foreleg up to the center of the bottom third, and you have a heart shot. If you shoot high or you shoot a couple of inches too far back, you still have a fatal shot in the lungs. But you have very little margin for error if you shoot low or too far forward.

In terms of effect, anticipate a frantic final run of possibly 75 yards with a heart shot. However, you can expect your deer to go down in its tracks if you use a fairly powerful rifle with a tough or heavy bullet and you break both shoulders while transiting the heart. Because of the very small margin for error, I don't like frontal shots; it's better to wait for the buck to turn, unless again, you are fairly close and very steady. The angle is dictated to some extent by the caliber you're using and the penetrating properties of your bullet. I don't like the so-called Texas heart shot on unwounded deer, but, especially if you're trophy hunting, I think it's wise to use enough gun and enough bullet that you can take any reasonable shot in terms of both range and presentation.

From this top view it really becomes obvious how small the heart and lungs are for a straight-on frontal shot. Also note, again from the top angle, how the heart is surrounded by the should blades and the spine.

Reprinted with permission of Safari Press from The Perfect Shot, North America.

Aging Whitetail on the Hoof

Dave Richards & Al Brothers

Photographs provided by Dave Richards

UNDER THE BEST OF CIRCUMSTANCES, AGING WHITE-TAILED deer on the hoof is a calculated guess. Even when all proper methods have been utilized and all available information analyzed, you will still make mistakes. It is also important to understand that every deer herd is unique and that numerous variables must be considered before you can consistently age deer on a particular property.

One factor to consider is how nutrition, or lack thereof, has affected the deer you are trying to age. Has there been an extended drought or periods of above-average rainfall that could have affected body and antler development? Other potential considerations include: How many years has the property been under management? Is the property high fenced or low fenced? Does the ranch feed high protein, and, if so, how long has the feeding program been in place? Does the ranch plant food plots and what do those plots contain? Any situations you can think of that could affect deer nutrition are pertinent. Different nutritional levels affect deer body growth and development and can cause variations among deer from different properties.

In most situations, deer herds provided high-quality, supplemental feeds have heavier body weights and larger antlers at younger ages than those relying solely on natural habitat. This is an important consideration when estimating age. Another major consideration is time of year. The characteristics we have focused on are best recognized during the rut. This focus is intentional, as hunting season typically occurs during the rut. A buck's body is on a physical roller coaster throughout the year, which greatly affects how old he appears. During the summer months, much of a mature buck's nutritional intake is directed to antler development and

There are several factors to take into account when aging whitetail deer on the hoof. One major consideration is time of year. The characteristics we have focused on are best recognized during the rut.

body growth, though his neck remains quite thin. In the fall, about the time he rubs the velvet from his antlers, his nutritional intake is directed to increasing muscle mass, particularly in his neck and chest as he prepares for the rut. This weight and muscle mass gain takes place in just eight to 10 weeks and can drastically alter how a buck appears. Later, as a buck participates in the rut by chasing does and fighting other bucks, he will lose the recently gained weight. By mid-January he will appear thin and often gaunt. Thus, the buck you got a glimpse of in mid-December that looked like a muscle-bound 5-½-year-old super buck may look like a typical 4-½-year-old by mid-January.

With the numerous variables involved, it is clear that trying to age a buck in a few critical seconds during a hunt is not a simple matter, and sometimes mistakes will occur. There are definitely bucks that are mature shooters and some that are immature nonshooters. However, there are a lot of 3-½- to 5-½-year-old-bucks- that, depending on season, lighting, distance, behavior, and body angle, can appear older than they really are. I have taken photographs of the same buck only seconds apart. Sometimes these photographs are only a few steps apart, and because of the lighting and the buck's hair being raised in response to another buck's presence, you would say he is a shooter. Then a few steps later he is a nonshooter. First impressions are why many bucks are taken before their time. Light, angle, and behavior affect how a buck appears. Often minute-by-minute changes in perception occur, especially if other bucks are present. This is when observation time can be your best friend or worst enemy. If you are in a rush while hunting, time will be your enemy, because you may rush the shot before making a fair judgment. However, if possible, allow time for the buck to approach closer and your adrenaline to slow. Then, start analyzing him, comparing him to other deer by body, antler characteristics, and behavior toward them. By doing so, the odds of making a correct decision turn rapidly in your favor.

When a buck approaches and other bucks are present, always be slower in your judgment of age. Many times a buck will come in with hair erect and appear much older. Let him relax and flatten his hair before judging. Often I have seen a buck appear 200 to 300 yards away and immediately think he is a big mature buck. He will appear dark and huge against the light-colored grass, and his slow swagger just adds to the false information my eyes are telling my brain. A few moments later another buck will be seen

There are numerous attributes to look for when aging a buck in the field—the neck/ brisket, skin under the chin, hair on the forehead, and the tarsal area. The photographs throughout this chapter demonstrate examples of each. Notice how the neck joins the brisket on the deer pictured above.

crossing the same sendero (a long clearing in thick brush) in close proximity to the first buck. The new buck doesn't seem to have the time to notice the first buck and moves on quickly. Then with the same speed of flipping an electrical switch the big, mature buck deflates. He lays his hair back down and immediately appears two years younger than first thought. This scenario describes how one buck's behavior toward another buck can fool you. Little Roy has told me on more than one occasion that they almost never shoot a deer the first time they see it unless it is a spike or unless they have someone with them who also knows deer and agrees it is a shooter.

AGING TIP

When a buck approaches and other bucks are present, always be slower in your judgment of age. Many times a buck will come in with hair erect and appear much older. Let him relax and flatten his hair before judging.

Then there are early mornings in predawn light. As I watch through my Leupold binoculars there is a dark shape that materializes like a ghost into the sendero. It is a huge-bodied whitetail with a lot of headgear that is feeding closer and closer. After several long minutes, the dark night begins to change to shades of gray, and the buck, which had appeared heavy horned and mature in the dark, loses two years and 20 inches of antler in a matter of 10 minutes. That is another of the many scenarios that can cause you to misjudge a buck's age.

The angle from which you are viewing a particular buck also can lead to an aging mistake. Most hunters are familiar with the statement, "You never age or judge a buck as he is going away from you." This angle makes a buck appear much bigger than he really is. However, going away is not the only angle that can deceive you. The angle that occurs when a buck's head is down and feeding often exaggerates the fullness of his stomach. Often how a buck postures with his head held high from straight-on can make him appear heavier and older. I have seen some big 4-½-year-olds from the frontal view that could trigger a wrong decision if a split second was all the time available. The frontal view can be useful to judge facial characteristics relative to age, but the best angle is from the side. The side angle is best for observing how the neck and brisket join, how full the stomach area is, and if the back is straight or sagging. However, it is always best to view the buck from multiple angles. The more time you can watch a buck from different

Another attribute to consider when aging a buck on the hoof is skin under the chin. In this photograph, the buck has loose neck skin.

Notice how the hair on the forehead gland appears. This buck's is noticeably thick and dark.

angles, analyze and put each piece of the puzzle together, the better your aging decision will be.

Distance is a variable that has a way of creating ground shrinkage once the trigger has been pulled. The closer you can observe deer the better. A good spotting scope and the best pair of binoculars you can afford are extremely important if you desire to minimize mistakes. High-quality optics will enable you to see the subtle details such as wrinkles under the chin, age in the face, thickening and graying of hair on the forehead, dimples in the neck and body, and the condition of the hocks. In recent times, there has been an increasing emphasis on shooting deer at longer distances. Attempting to judge deer at 200 yards or more without extremely good optics is poor judgment and preparation. In the past few years, binoculars and spotting scopes have been continually improved. A very good pair of binoculars can be purchased for $250 to $500, and a good spotting scope can be purchased for $200 to $900. The bottom line is that good optics are essential for anyone seriously interested in aging deer.

KNOW YOUR BUCKS

It's very important to be able to identify individual bucks from an early age. While antler shape can be helpful, be sure to key in on the characteristics of the face and body—variations in coloring, unique markings, throat patch configuration, etc.

If the first time you observe a deer he is 5-½ or older, you will have a very difficult time trying to determine an exact age. You will run into difficulties many times during the hunting season, but the more bucks you can identify on sight and become familiar with the sooner more of your bucks will start living to 6-½ and 7-½ years old. In fact, the earlier you can recognize a particular buck and correctly age him, the more accurate you will be, and the more successful your management program will be.

People often look incredulous when I talk about a specific buck I have observed over a period of years. Yet if I ask them whether they have any trouble identifying their friends on a regular basis the answer is always a resounding no. The shortcoming is that most landowners and hunters have not spent enough time looking closely at deer to pick out individual characteristics to help identify them later.

The key to identifying individual bucks is to carefully scrutinize each one you see, regardless of age or size. While antler shape and size can be helpful, facial and body characteristics are more reliable, especially after age three. Look for any unique markings or features. Are the ears black-tipped or brown? Are there big white eye patches or almost no eye patches at all? Is a white throat patch present, and what shape is it? Is the throat patch round or rectangular? Is the throat patch distinct or faded? Is there a double throat patch? Are there any unusual body colorations? Is there a dark stripe of hair down the neck or back? Are extremely white forelegs present making it appear as if he is wearing socks? What color is the top of the tail? Is it solid brown or solid black? Is part of the tail missing? Some bucks' tails appear as if they have been partially dipped in black while others have more white surrounding the entire tail.

WANT MORE?

The complete narrative by Dave Richards and co-author Al Brothers is available in the book *Observing and Evaluating Whitetails*, published in 2003. You can pick up a hardcover copy for $39.95 from the Quality Deer Management Association on their web site www.qdma.com, or by calling (800-209-3337). The full-length book includes more information on aging, behavior, antler development, all beautifully illustrated with hundreds of color photographs.

Next, focus on the face. What color are the eyes? Are they extremely dark, appearing black, or are they very light, causing the eyes to take on an amber appearance? Do the eyes appear close or far apart? Are the eyes slanted, making it appear as if he is squinting, or is he wide-eyed, giving the appearance the eyes are bulging out? Are the ears held up or laid flat? Does one ear droop? Is there a tear, hole, or gap in the ear? Does the face appear long or short and stubby? Is there a pointed, dainty nose, a Roman nose, or a wide, flat nose? How is the head held when standing? Is it held high as if surveying the country? Some bucks have this trait. What about the gait? Some bucks can be identified by their peculiar walking gait even from a distance. Most bucks will have one or more identifiable markings or characteristics that will enable positive identification.

Throughout this chapter are several bucks I have photographed over the years that have easily-identifiable features. Look them over and see how well you pick up their unique features that distinguish them from other bucks. This will be good practice for recognizing individual bucks on your own property or lease in the future.

A major attribute to look for is condition of a buck's tarsal area. Take note of the degree of staining on this deer.

BUCK FAWNS

It is important not to mistake buck fawns for mature does. They are this year's fawns and usually still with their mothers early in the season. Note the small nubs barely visible on their heads. A good spotting scope or pair of binoculars is a must to identify these young bucks. Look at the length of the head — it will be shorter and more compact than older deer. Also, look at the shape of the forehead. Buck fawns have flat foreheads while does have rounded foreheads. This feature becomes more pronounced later in the season. Buck fawns often are separated from their mothers during the breeding season and commonly observed traveling and feeding alone. These young bucks are often the first deer to appear at a feeding area or food plot. Thus, it is wise to never shoot a lone antlerless deer, especially at long distances. Always ensure other antlerless deer are present to allow a size comparison.

1-½-YEAR-OLDS

As you can see, 1-½-year-old bucks appear dainty with baby faces and thin necks. Their legs appear long and slender, and their torso is slim like a doe's. In a photo of a 1-½-year-old buck, cover the antlers with your thumb and you will see that the body resembles a doe. Yearling buck antler development is highly variable, ranging from tiny spikes to 10 or more points. But, even super 1-½-year-old bucks with multiple points will have small, thin antlers. Likewise, regardless of the number of points, the length of their main beams will be short compared to older bucks. Their tarsal area will be small and lightly colored. Some 1-½-year-old bucks will still be traveling with their mothers into the rut, but most will have dispersed. It is at this age that many relocate and establish separate home ranges from their mothers.

2-½-YEAR-OLDS

The best way to describe the bodies of 2-½-year-old bucks is gangly and awkward. Their legs appear to be growing too fast for their body. Their bodies, while thicker than those of 1-½-year-olds, still have legs and necks that appear stretched in proportion. Their back and stomach area will appear very taut, and their face appears larger than their thin neck from a frontal view. The head will appear long from the side. For the first time, their antlers will begin to catch your eye, which is probably why 2-½ is the average age of whitetail bucks harvested in many areas. The truth is their antlers are just starting to grow. Most 2-½-year-olds are big travelers during the rut, because they typically are not active breeders in herds with balanced adult sex ratios and good buck age structure. Lack of breeding is not from lack of desire but due to competition and dominance from older bucks. During the rut their tarsal glands may be dark, but the very darkest area is usually very small and round in appearance.

3-½-YEAR-OLDS

A fuller neck and deeper chest are characteristics of a 3-½-year-old. As the bucks pictured demonstrate, their neck muscles are expanding from increased hormones and use during the rut but are still not as large or thick as a fully-mature buck. Their chest is beginning to appear larger than their rump, but their back and stomach are still straight and taut. Also, their neck is still distinct by four or five inches from their brisket. Their tarsals will be dark during the rut but usually will appear small, and the dark staining from urine usually does not extend down the leg to the hoof.

4-½-YEAR-OLDS

When bucks reach 4-½ they attain skeletal maturity and begin exhibiting many characteristics of full maturity. Their rump will appear full and rounded. Their neck will be more muscular and their body thicker and fuller but still trim. Their stomach and back will not appear to sag, and their jaw skin will be tight. This is the first time their legs do not appear longer than they should for their body. Their legs may even appear slightly short for the thickened body. During the rut, their tarsals will be noticeably large and dark due to repeated urinating and rubbing. In many respects, 4-½-year-old bucks are similar to young athletes in their early 20s. Their bodies have reached full size but are muscular and lean. The majority of 4-½-year-old bucks will have a significant increase in antler growth over the previous

year. For the first time, much of the nutritional intake is directed to antler growth instead of muscle and skeletal growth. Bucks at this age can grow very respectable antlers making them difficult for hunters to pass. Focus your attention on the body and face when aging, especially if the buck has very good antlers. Typically, 4-½-year-olds breed more does than any other age class. This is because they are in prime physical condition and quite competitive in the dominance hierarchy.

5-½-YEAR-OLDS

At 5-½ years old, most bucks will be carrying the largest set of antlers they have ever grown. Their bodies also exhibit some noticeable changes. Typically, their stomach and back have a noticeable sag. Their neck will swell considerably during the rut, making the neck and brisket appear to be one continuous muscle. Also, their neck, while being very big, will appear muscular and firm and not flabby. The tarsals will be noticeably large and very dark with many bucks having staining down the inside of the leg to the hoof. Late in the rut their legs may even appear slightly white under the tarsals where the urine has scalded their hide. Also at 5-½, the forehead gland appears noticeably thicker and darker because of increased secretions from the specialized sweat glands underneath. Finally, 5-½-year-old bucks' legs will appear short almost to an exaggerated extent, due to the fuller and fatter bodies.

6-½-YEAR-OLDS

At 6-½ years old, there is no doubt a buck is mature. During the rut, their neck will often be almost as thick as their body and will connect to their brisket as if one, continuous muscle. Their face will appear small in proportion to the thickness of their neck from a frontal view. Their body will be heavy and appear rippled, especially in the chest and neck areas. Throughout most of the year they will have a sagging stomach, except during the post-rut due to weight loss. Their back will also sag, making their front shoulders appear taller. The hair patch on their forehead is noticeably thicker and darker, and the chin will show ripples and may sag. Their tarsals and lower inside legs will be darkly stained down to the hoof. Late in the rut, they may have a large, grayish-white area under the tarsal where it has been scalded from urine. Finally, many bucks this age will have testicles that appear larger and descended lower than normal.

7-½-YEAR-OLDS

The bodies of 7-½-year-old bucks appear huge. If they appear with younger deer, especially younger bucks, they will almost appear as a larger subspecies. Their bodies will have wrinkles and dimples, and their stomachs and backs will sag. During the rut their necks will be so thick it is difficult to determine where they stop and their briskets begin. If moving, their necks will appear flabby instead of firm like those of 5-½-year-olds. Often, the skin under the chin will sag. In the fall, their faces and the hair on the forehead gland will appear gray. However, as the rut approaches, their forehead will usually become darker due to secretions from the forehead

gland. Their legs will appear short because their bodies are so large. During the rut, their tarsals will be very large with dark staining extending down the lower inside leg to the hoof. Late in the rut they may have large, grayish-white, scalding under the tarsals that are larger than the tarsal itself. Their testicles will be noticeably large and descended quite low. Many bucks will have their greatest antler mass at this age. Some will grow more total points and non-typical points, although the typical tines may be slightly shorter than at 5-½. Many 7-½-year-old bucks appear to have a rigid, slow gait when walking, showing the stiffness in their joints that is indicative of older age.

POST MATURITY

While some bucks grow sizable antlers at or beyond 8-½ years of age, most wildlife managers in south Texas consider 7-½ the best age to harvest bucks if antler size is the primary consideration. Beyond 7-½ years of age, there also is an increasing chance of loss from natural mortality. Interestingly, as bucks pass 7-½ they can become quite a challenge to hunt unless you have patterned and can identify the particular buck. As bucks reach old age their teeth can become badly worn, resulting in reduced nutritional intake and an overall decline in condition. Often, their bodies will resemble those of 3-½-year-olds with slimmer bodies and necks. The only clues may be a graying scalp and face and slightly-protruding hip and rib bones. Post-mature bucks will often display knocked knees, noticeably-sagging stomachs, and swayed backs with a hump above the shoulders. Also, their rumps appear more pointed than rounded as they were in prime years. They often are very stiff-legged and slow, showing their old bodies and joints are wearing out. Their antlers will usually decrease in overall size and mass. When the teeth are badly worn, the antlers and body can deteriorate rapidly. Some very old bucks produce antler points that curl or appear crooked as if they were melted in a fire. Often, they will shed their antlers earlier than other bucks. Watching a buck as he relates to other mature bucks will often help determine whether he is post-mature. If he acts submissive to younger 4-½- to 7-½-year-olds, and all the physical characteristics of post maturity are present, his prime years have already passed.

AGE-CLASS POP QUIZ

Think you have aging on the hoof figured out? Let's give it a shot. Can you identify the body characteristics that differentiate the age classes?

Left 1-½, Right 2-½

Left 4-½, Right 3-½

Left 5-½, Right 3-½

Left 2-½, Right 6-½

Left 3-55, Right 7-45

Whitetail Hunting—
Tactics, Techniques and Insights
From Experts Across North America

WE HAVE COMPILED AN ALL-STAR CAST TO PROVIDE YOU WITH a variety of hunting tactics, techniques, and insights to help improve your whitetail hunting experience. These gentlemen hail from Texas to Canada and numerous states in between, covering a broad range of habits and hunting methods.

They represent seasoned veterans whose adventures appear on TV and the pages of today's best hunting magazines to standout individuals who don't work in the outdoor industry but have proven track records with multiple records-book whitetails in B&C's Big Game Records Program amongst them. This vast array of experience will help you think outside the box and pick up several tips along the way that you can implement in your own neck of the woods. There is more than one way to hunt whitetails, and these authors provide real-world strategies and success stories!

Searching for sheds in the off-season is an excellent tactic for verifying what caliber deer the property you are hunting may hold. Read more in Glen Salow's section beginning on page 178.

TAKEN BY:
JERRY BRYANT
NOV 13 2001
FULTON CO. IL
F D WT 233 LBS
BC SCORE 291 1/8
TAXIDERMY
BY
RON MEINDERS

This Way to Paradise

Gordon Whittington | Editor, *North American Whitetail*

Is THERE SOME RELIABLE ROAD MAP TO SHOOTING A BOONE and Crockett whitetail? If so, I'd throw money at its owner until he sold it to me. Then I'd print truckloads of copies and make a fortune. Millions of avid whitetail hunters would be eager to buy one.

Even in a poor season, the number of B&C whitetails bagged somewhere on the continent ends up well north of 500. Far more North Americans can claim a B&C trophy of this species than any other. Even so, the number of such sportsmen pales in comparison to the throngs who have yet to tag one. And the total number of folks who have shot more than one record whitetail is almost microscopic.

What separates the haves from the have-nots in this crowd? Are they following some magical map others aren't? Not really. Even here in the Information Age, no such map exists. Nor does any other exact process guaranteed to produce records-book results. You can do everything right and still strike out on B&C bucks for an entire career. You also can seemingly do everything "wrong" and shoot one.

But that's not to say the would-be trophy taker must depend totally on providence to bring him or her a great whitetail. Some factors we of course do control, or at least influence, in the quest for success.

In my nearly three decades at *North American Whitetail*, I've befriended many hunters whose names dot the B&C listings. I've worked closely with hundreds of them to help them tell their stories in print, online and on television. I've sifted through thousands of their photos, as well as score charts, aerial photos, maps and whatever else I could to gain a better understanding of records-book success. And on a few special occasions, I've

Being in the right place at the right time, whether or not your looking for a trophy whitetail makes all the difference. Jerry D. Bryant took this beauty of a non-typical whitetail in 2003 while turkey hunting! The buck scores 304-3/8 points and is the third largest non-typical entered in the Club's Records Program.

even walked with these hunters to the very spots in which they experienced their glorious moments in the sun.

After all those years of working with successful trophy hunters, and even having hunted the species myself in more than 40 states and provinces of North America (plus New Zealand and Finland), I don't claim to have any secrets about big bucks nailed down. But certain truths about the quest for a B&C whitetail have become evident to me after all these years in the woods and at the editor's desk.

GEOGRAPHY

Of course, first among the many factors affecting trophy success is location. Nothing else matters nearly as much.

Many hunting properties in the whitetail's range contain no bucks large enough to make the book. Zero. In such places, even if a buck is huge by local standards, he might not even be close to B&C class. I'm convinced that if we look at the 10-million-plus folks who hunt whitetails in a given year, most never have seen a live "book" whitetail in the flesh. And most taxidermists never have mounted one.

Many counties with good numbers of whitetails have yielded no qualifying bucks to date. It doesn't necessarily mean they never will—it just means they haven't. On the other hand, a few have produced so many that if a season passes without one turning up, it's honestly a shock to the locals.

There's a fine balance in putting numbers of bucks into the records book. To have a fighting chance of reaching B&C size, even a genetically gifted buck must live several years and receive decent nourishment. Agriculture works in favor of supplying enough of the right groceries. But intensive agriculture also tends to mean little security cover, accompanied by lower deer numbers and often, worse age structure. Farmland deer thus need some protection from pressure, whether through firearms restrictions, reduced hunter density, non-rut gun hunting and/or antler restrictions.

Is the average whitetail hunter in one whitetail state or province really much more skilled than his or her counterpart somewhere else? Certain skills between any two groups of hunters will vary, due largely to habitats and hunting restrictions. A serious whitetail hunter from northern Idaho likely is better at snow-tracking bucks than is a swamper from Louisiana; a hardcore South Texas *sendero* hunter should be a more confident 300-yard rifleman than an avid Delaware slug aficionado. But can that explain why one province cranks out 20 or more B&C racks a year, while another is doing well to record two? Of course not. There's way more to it than skill, or even the sheer number of hunters afield.

Peruse a continental map color-coded by numbers of B&C qualifiers produced (See the Reference Section on page 232). If luck is the overriding key to killing a book whitetail, it's inequitably distributed. There must be a far greater number of lucky hunters in Pike County, Ohio, and Pike County, Illinois, than in Pike County, Georgia. And while Alberta has far fewer deer hunters than does Alabama, on average they're many times more fortunate in taking trophies.

The simple fact is that luck, as it is loosely defined in trophy hunting, is more regularly enjoyed where there are more big animals available. I'm arguably twice as good a trophy hunter in an area containing twice as many trophy bucks.

So in some ways, my earlier road map analogy perhaps is fairly apt after all. Roads that lead to the right places—or away from the wrong ones, if you prefer—really are worth finding and following if a record whitetail is your goal.

THE RIGHT STRATEGY

Not that many years ago, even in the more open country of the Midwest, the Great Plains and Canada's Prairie Provinces, when a record buck was shot, it was without prior knowledge of the animal—at least, without prior knowledge on the part of the person shooting him. A farmer might have seen the deer in a summer bean field, or a ranch hand might have jumped him while rounding up cattle, but for the most part, the final encounter was a shock. A man, woman or child went hunting, and a monster buck more or less fell from the sky, landing on the person's wall and in the records book. It all seemed quite miraculous and with little context: a singular event often described as, for lack of anything more appropriate, pure luck.

Some people seemingly can find a winning lottery ticket lying on a busy sidewalk. In much the same sense, the occasional hunter can wander into the woods without knowing Boone and Crockett from Laurel and Hardy but end up looking like an expert down at the check station.

One hunter of my acquaintance wasn't even going after deer the day he took a world-class whitetail. He had a fall turkey permit and had carried his crossbow out in search of a big turkey gobbler known to roam a friend's property. The hunter climbed into the old wooden tree stand and—after spooking off the turkey he was trying to kill—shot one of the greatest non-typical whitetails of all time. The monster had chased a doe to within 15 yards of the tree that mid-November day.

Another hunter I know shot a B&C whitetail because he couldn't walk. (The hunter, I mean, not the deer.) The guy's back had locked up on him in the course of a day conducting late-season drives with friends. Unable to make it even to a nearby creek bottom to wait in ambush, he told the rest of the party he'd just sit out the last drive of the day. But another hunter convinced him to just stand there in a fencerow while other posters went to the good spots and the drivers began a final push. Guess what ran to within 15 yards of the hunter who could scarcely even walk? A typical that grossed nearly 200 inches and netted nearly 190. (He did tell me it was several hours following the kill before he thought about his back again.)

Perhaps there's no full explanation of how those two guys stumbled into shooting world-class whitetails at 15 yards while many trophy addicts never get within howitzer range of one. But two undeniable facts held true in each of those examples: (1) The hunter was on land holding at least one B&C buck; and (2) when the chance to shoot such a deer presented itself—serendipitously though it might have been—the guy made good on it. Those are elements we as hunters can at least somewhat control.

Another, of course, is narrowing down the area being hunted. Today, more than ever before, a fair percentage of B&C bucks are known to someone before the kill. That's mainly because even casual hunters now often employ scouting trail cameras, especially as the season approaches. Many avid whitetailers keep multiple units in the woods nonstop. Because of this ongoing surveillance, at some point even the most secretive buck can blunder into having his portrait made. It might be at 2:14 a.m. in July or at 12:58 p.m. in November, but at some point he's likely to be discovered. And at that point, the pursuit kicks up a notch.

No other technological advancement has had this great an impact on trophy whitetail success. Firearms, ammunition and optics of course keep improving, letting us see and shoot with greater accuracy at greater range. Innovation in archery gear has boosted performance in bow seasons even more. Yet regardless of optics or shooting gear, nothing else can matter unless the hunter is within the right deer's home range. The scouting camera

First among the many factors affecting trophy success is location. Nothing else matters nearly as much. Makes sense—if the area your hunting doesn't have a trophy whitetail living on it, you'll be hard pressed to shoot one. Saskatchewan grain and cattle farmer, Milo Hanson, had heard reports that this incredible buck was on his property before they took to the field. His deer has reigned as the World's Record since 1993 with a score of 213-5/8 points.

is what's helping more hunters get into that magical zone of potential success by design, rather than by chance.

Of course, even after zeroing in on the right place to hunt, most sportsmen strike out on B&C whitetails. They never shoot one—or even *at* one. So what, beyond finding the home range of a qualifying buck, really matters?

Timing, for one thing. Largely due to that trail camera surveillance, it's becoming more common for B&C bucks to be taken by bow in late summer/early fall. There's now an annual flurry of such kills around the bow opener, whenever that is in a given area. Not so many years ago, we seldom saw this. In fact, many trophy enthusiasts didn't even get serious about buck hunting until late in the pre-rut. Now many focus on a few days of hunting a specific trophy buck when the season starts. If they shoot him, great; if not, they back out of his core area until it's time for enhanced daylight movement related to breeding.

The simple fact is that luck, as it is loosely defined in trophy hunting, is more regularly enjoyed where there are more big animals available. I'm arguably twice as good a trophy hunter in an area containing twice as many trophy bucks. Buffalo County, Wisconsin, has more B&C whitetail entries than any other county in the U.S. Elliot Smith harvested this Buffalo County B&C buck in 2012.

While rattling, calling, mock scrapes and decoying all have become popular ways to take advantage of a buck's breeding urges, they still don't contribute to the demise of most B&C-class whitetails. The majority are shot as they're looking for or trailing does. That means knowing when the rut will hit in a given area still very much matters. It remains the sweetest part of the season for big deer.

Another recent trend in the whitetail world is the increased use of food plots. Although often touted as addressing deer health and other management concerns, most receive some hunting pressure. Good plots concentrate deer activity, making them of particular benefit to small landowners in the Midwest and Great Lakes regions. Trophy bowhunters in particular have benefited from this trend, arrowing many B&C bucks in or around such plots.

MIND GAMES

Relative to the pursuit of most other big game species, hunting trophy whitetails is a sedentary pastime. You pick a stand site and wait. And wait. And wait some more.

This waiting, of course, leaves you plenty of time to think—which can lead to second-guessing, which more often than not leads to nothing good.

The mental game is where some deer hunters blow away the competition. They aren't necessarily using better gear or tactics than the next guy. They aren't always even hunting better land. Their real edge lies in confidence. They know they've done their homework and have forged a good plan. And they know if they can just stick with it, there's a good chance it will pay off. Maybe not today, or tomorrow, or even next month. But eventually.

Confidence greatly boosts patience, one of the most pivotal components of trophy whitetail success. It tends to matter every step of the way. First, there's the patience to keep scouting for the best possible stand sites. Then the patience to wait for the right conditions to hunt. Then the patience to keep hunting. Often, somewhere along the way, the hunter also will need the patience to pass up a lesser buck while waiting on Mr. Big. Of course, when that B&C contender finally steps out, there's often a need for patience to wait for just the right shot. And finally, in many cases, a hunter needs patience to wait to take up the trail to his or her shot buck to maximize the chances of finding the trophy. Patience pervades the entire process.

CONCLUSION

Faithfully adhering to the points mentioned above should improve a hunter's chances of someday taking a B&C buck. But there are no guarantees doing so will result in victory. Then again, ignoring them won't guarantee failure, either. As noted, some record kills seemingly are just meant to be. However, even they tend to follow certain patterns if we dig deeply enough to find them. Deciphering those patterns, then being persistent and skilled enough to capitalize on the rare chances afforded is often what separates the whitetail hunter with a B&C entry from all the rest.

Older is Easier
Bill Winke | Outdoor Writer & TV Personality

IT IS A WELL-HELD BELIEF THAT AS A BUCK GETS OLDER HE GETS smarter. They become like ghosts that know what hunters are going to do before they even do it. These bucks slip around us, never seen. Surely, you learned these irrefutable truths when you started deer hunting. I know the message was beaten into my head. It was logical and explained why I came up short in tagging the giants, so I bought that line for many years.

The light has finally shined in through my fog and I don't believe it any longer. My experiences with hunting only mature bucks for the past dozen years tells me that they are not really any smarter than bucks a few years their junior. If you are hunting carefully and not seeing mature bucks, it is for one of two reasons: either they are not there or they are moving only at night.

Furthermore, I have learned another interesting fact: as bucks become old, they actually become easier to kill!

I am not the only person who has noticed this. I hear it from almost everyone I talk to who is fortunate enough to hunt areas where bucks can reach full maturity. Intense camera scouting and selective hunting practices that target only older bucks have been on the increase over the past 20 years. The result is a new wealth of information pointing toward errors in the old paradigm between hunter and hunted.

Personalities and behavior of bucks do change as they mature. Their ranges get smaller and they become more daylight active within those areas. Debunking the conventional wisdom that old bucks are ghosts is the goal of this article. If nothing else, my message should bring hope to your whitetail hunting. I know it has sure changed the way I approach the game.

A buck I shot in late November of 2013. This deer was fully mature and daylight active. The evening I shot him he was out feeding well over an hour before sunset!

MAKING MY CASE

This isn't something I dreamed up one night after eating too much spicy food. On my farm, my friends and I have encountered, and killed, some surprisingly dumb-acting bucks over the years; all of them ended up being six years old or older. In fact, I have never hunted a buck that didn't get easier to kill when he got past age six. We get the bucks on this farm professionally aged by a lab that sections the incisors, so we aren't guessing on the ages of these deer. Plus, most of them are bucks I know very well from sightings and trail camera photos dating back to their younger days.

I understand how few people ever get to hunt old bucks, but this is all about conservation, restraint and management. I am hoping that a good number of you have had this privilege, or at least plan to start passing younger bucks in the future.

BUCKS I HAVE KNOWN

On my farm, we have killed six bucks in the last five seasons that were six years old, or older. We have hunted a few others in that category that died of other causes during that same time. To be fair, there have been other

6+ year old bucks here that we didn't see all the that often, but also never actually hunted them.

Here is a summary of the life cycles of several of these old bucks. I think you will start to see a pattern develop.

Stickers: In 2008, my friend Mike Sawyer made hay on my farm, killing two old monarchs. The first was on November 12 when he shot a buck that we had nicknamed

OPPOSITE: Mike Sawyer with "Stickers", a buck he shot on the author's farm early one afternoon in November of 2008. This buck was a very daylight active buck and was at least 6 years old based on body and other aging cues.

ABOVE: Mike Sawyer with the second buck he shot on the author's farm during the 2008 season (this one falling in early January 2009). It is another very old buck that was active in full daylight and not acting wary despite the fact that Sawyer and his cousin had already shot deer from the stand over the two previous evenings.

Stickers. This old deer was an absolute beast, with a huge body and head and many sticker points at the bases of his antlers. I saw Stickers at mid-morning four days before and from a stand ¾ of a mile away from where Mike shot him.

Mike shot the buck in the middle of the afternoon as the deer was out cruising. This daylight roamer seemed almost nonchalant in his movements, not showing any caution as he strolled around the farm.

Giant 8: Mike's second monster that season fell on January 3, 2009. We had never seen this buck prior to the evening he stepped out and had no photos of him. I don't know anything about him other than the fact that he was a giant and he was moving in the middle of the afternoon.

On top of that, Mike and his cousin had already killed three does and a buck from that stand in the past two evenings. There were blood trails and human scent aplenty. The buck couldn't have been particularly wary or he wouldn't have overlooked all that scent. He was a total surprise—I think attracted to the spot by the alfalfa field that the stand overlooked.

58°F   10/25/09 06:07 PM   5555555555

The "Great 8" in 2009. I had sheds and summer video footage of this buck for a few years before he finally changed his habits and became daylight active. I believe he was at least 6 years old in 2009, and he may have been a year or two older yet. After studying the trail cam photos of the buck, I figured out where he must be living and when the wind was right moved in. On October 30, 2009, I called him to 30 but made a bad shot when he ducked the string. He died late that winter.

High-Low: My neighbor named this buck. Scott was seeing High-Low all the time in November of 2009 and had passed him several times. But the buck was also very daylight active on my farm, as evidenced by the many trail cam photos we had of him. In early December, the buck walked right past the blind where our son, me and a cameraman were sitting. The three of us were bumbling around like the Three Stooges, swinging open doors and windows, knocking over the heater, dropping a cell phone, getting burned—in general, making a racket.

The buck never even looked our way as he passed at 30 yards. I was

Drew Winke with a buck nicknamed "High Low" that he shot in December of 2009. This buck was very visible and didn't display cautious behavior. He ended up being 8 years old when the tooth analysis came back from the lab.

shocked. Our son, Drew, killed him at 40 yards on the other side of the blind after we stopped laughing. The tooth analysis on this buck marked him as an eight year old.

Jamie: I hunted a buck from 2006 through 2010 that I called "Jamie". He was already mature when I found him. I saw him twice in daylight that first year but not again until 2010 though he was on my trail cameras nearly every night during that time. The buck was strictly nocturnal in 2008 and 2009 but in 2010, he was quite the opposite. I finally killed the old buck on November 22, 2010 just 150 yards from the house—the third time I had seen him that season and the second time within bow range. He was also eight years old.

Neither of these old bucks were particularly big-antlered, but both were prized trophies because they were ancient. Their age made them trophies. But more to the point, their age also made them complacent—possibly comfortable—but certainly much easier to kill.

8 47°F ◐ 10/24/09 10:02 PM 5555555555

DLCcovert.com   12.04.2009 7:17:18

Two images of "Jamie" in 2009. To my knowledge, this buck was totally nocturnal in 2008 and 2009 when he was 5 and 6 years old. I hunted where he lived often and monitored cameras in those areas but never got a single daylight photo or saw the buck.

This is what "Jamie" looked like when I shot him in late November 2010. After never seeing him on the hoof for two full seasons, he was fairly visible in 2010. Tooth aging pegged him at 7 years old in 2010.

Great 8: This buck was at least six years old, possibly much older. I had three sets of sheds from him and he was the same size all three years—already big. I would guess he was a gross 160-inch eight pointer—pretty darn nice. But most interestingly, he had an absolute giant body. The Great 8 was ghost from 2006-2008 and then all of a sudden in 2009 he started to show up regularly on my trail camera in daylight.

He always approached it in the afternoons from the direction of a brushy draw. That was likely where he was bedding. Finally, the wind was right on Halloween to hunt a stand near the ditch. The Great 8 came to my grunt call about an hour after daylight that morning and I skipped an arrow off his back when he dropped at the sound of the shot. Ugh, three years of searching botched! He died that winter, presumably from old age.

HOW THEY CHANGE

Now that I have warmed you up a little, I am going to drill down into

DLCcovert.com   4.02.2009 12:22:17

Bushnell   09-27-2012 18:42:56

OPPOSITE TOP: This is the "Double G4 Buck" in October 2010. The date on the photo is wrong. Is there any wonder the buck grabbed my attention to the point where I hunted only that deer for the entire season. The buck was 5 years old that season and I never saw him in daylight nor did I get any daylight photos of him despite spending nearly 70 days hunting him that season!

ABOVE: The "Double G4 Buck" in 2011. He had blown up into a giant that year and as a 6-year-old, was all over that ridge in full daylight. Often, he was the first deer to come out in the evening. What a change from his behavior in 2010! I had him within 40 yards three times with my bow that season but failed to close the deal!

OPPOSITE BOTTOM: "Double G4 Buck" in 2012. As a seven-year-old, the buck was all over the area in daylight. Each year that I hunted this buck his range continued to shrink. I believe that by 2012 he was mostly living in an area no larger than about 30 acres!

Here is what "Double G4" looked like in 2012 when I shot him on November 3. He was seven years old that year and was the most patternable buck on the entire farm. The way his behavior and personality changed from age 5 to age 6 was truly remarkable.

the annual story of two more old bucks I recently hunted. I have a lot of detail on these two and knew them very well. I killed both during the 2012 season and both were 7 years old.

One I named "Double G4" and the other was "Loppy". Not surprisingly, their names came from their early antler characteristics. I was aware of Double G4 when he was a 140 gross inch 3 year old, but I didn't start hunting him until the next year. I first learned of Loppy in 2009.

2009: Both bucks lived on the same ridge. I am guessing they were both four years old. G4 was a mid-160s buck and Loppy had weak side— just a cool buck, not a high scoring deer.

I saw both bucks three times that year and got a number of trail cam photos of them. I was trying to kill them both, but they made it through.

2010: Both were five years old. Double G4 was still living more or less on the same ridge and was a high 170's grossing buck. I got two photos

CLOCKWISE FROM TOP LEFT: "Loppy" in 2009, when I first started hunting him. I believe he was 4 years old that year. Notice that the weak side of his rack swapped sides in subsequent years—an interesting sidebar on the story of the hunt for this buck. | This is "Loppy" in October 2010. (The date on the photo is wrong). He grew a really cool brow tine that year—the only year he grew it—and he moved about a 1/4 mile to the west from where I had been seeing him in 2009. Though I hunted his area a lot that season, he never showed in daylight and never produced one daylight photo that year. He was likely 5 years old in 2010. | "Loppy" in 2011. He had moved another 1/4 mile to the west from where I had found him 2010 but he remained nocturnal to the best of my knowledge. He would have been at least 6 years old in 2011. | "Loppy" in 2012. He never showed up in daylight (on camera or in the field) that season despite the fact that the

author ran camera here for several weeks and hunted this area often. Loppy moved his range progressively 1/4 mile to the west each year from 2009 until Winke killed him in 2012.

RIGHT: What "Loppy" looked like when I finally killed him in late December 2012. It was the first time I had seen him during the hunting season since 2009! He was at least 7 years old that year.

The first buck I shot in 2013 (mid-October) was a 7-year-old we had named "Curly". He was very daylight active that year based on trail cam photos and I shot him well before sunset the first time I went in to hunt him.

of him all fall, both at night. Loppy had moved about a quarter-mile to the west where I got several nighttime trail cam photos of him. No daylight sightings of either buck though I hunted G4 (and the general area of Loppy) relentlessly all season.

2011: Now they are six years old. G4 had blown up into a monster, grossing 205 inches as a giant 6x5. He was still living on the same ridge. Loppy looked pretty much the same but he had moved another quarter-mile to the west—now a half mile from where I started hunting him in 2009.

Loppy remained nocturnal in 2011, but G4 was just the opposite. He was all over that field on the top of the ridge in broad daylight. Often, he was the first buck out in the afternoon. The transformation in his behavior was shocking—a true 180-degree turnaround from age five to age six.

It was an eventful late season as I zeroed in on G4. I put a blind on the ridge field in mid-December and by the end of the month, he had accepted it and was back to his daylight activities. I had him within 40 yards three times that season. I messed up twice and once he got lucky. Loppy remained a no-show.

2012: I killed both of these bucks in 2012. Both were seven years old. G4 grossed around 206, Loppy wasn't a buck you would score. I am proud of them both. The hunts were a lot of fun—as you might imagine—but I will save those for another day. The real story is how their personalities and behavior continued to change.

Loppy moved again, at least another quarter-mile west. So, by 2012, he was nearly a mile from where I started hunting him in 2009. G4 didn't budge one inch. In fact, he became even more entrenched. When I killed him on November 3, he was coming out on the same ridge where I first saw him in 2009! He remained highly visible that entire fall and his range continued to shrink. Based on my trail camera photos, he was living in an area of roughly 30 acres. Talk about shooting fish in a barrel!

Despite his giant antlers, G4 was the easiest buck I have ever hunted. I doubt there was a 1½ year old buck on the farm that would have been more predictable or more daylight active than this seven year old monster!

To my knowledge, we never educated that buck, at least not in a way that was able to learn I was after him. So he never had a decidedly negative experience with people. It pays to be careful, but it pays even more to be lucky enough to have a buck with that kind of genetics and that kind of personality living on your farm.

I killed Loppy on December 21. It took a cold front to bring him out in daylight. Thirty minutes later, I got a nice, clean 25-yard shot. It was the first time I had seen Loppy in daylight since 2009. For two seasons, he was totally nocturnal as far as I know. I am sure he moved back in the timber, but he never came near any of my cameras (mostly on field edges) in daylight those two years.

CONCLUSIONS

I can tell more stories about bucks like the ones I just described. In fact, during the 2013 season I shot two more old bucks. One was a 7 year old named Curly that was very daylight active in a small area. I killed him the first time I hunted him in mid-October. The other buck was a late rut kill as he was settling in on food sources. Again, he was an old deer moving in broad daylight.

If you pursue just one buck long enough you will come to realize that they are fascinating in their transformations, but there is nothing truly mystical about them. They live long lives by staying hidden in daylight and then, like the flipping of a switch, their behavior can totally change. I love making the hunt personal; to have the thrill of following the buck through his many changes knowing that at the end of the line, he will likely become much easier to hunt.

Success is Sometimes a Five-Letter Word...THINK

Larry L. Weishuhn | Wildlife Biologist, Outdoor Writer

"No señor, el macho grande, he no třevel in day... en noche!" Raising his hand toward his head he continued, "Hees muy viejo! Heem hab mucho břains!" With that, the vaquero took a long swallow of steaming hot coffee he had boiled over an open flame. "Caře caffee?"

I nodded an affirmative and watched the grizzled cowboy pour the boiling hot and black elixir into a blue enameled mug. Reaching for it I was glad I was wearing leather gloves. Blowing steam from the mug's surface, I looked up and asked, "Rafael, how should I hunt him?" referring to the buck he had describe as having "catořce" (14) typical points.

"No cometa en campo poř diaz, señor Colorado!" I nodded. I understood. It would be good to hunt during the middle of the day while others were in camp having lunch.

As a wildlife biologist who established and maintained quality deer management programs on a good part of the South Texas Brush Country and elsewhere while doing hundreds of helicopter game surveys, I had seen three typical 14-point bucks out of more than 100,000 whitetail bucks in the process. Thus, when the ranch cowboy, in whom I had great trust, told me of the 14-point typical, it piqued my interest.

I started hunting the buck early in the season, knowing quite often the best time to take a buck—especially one you know something about—is the earliest legal opportunity. This is while they are still somewhat in the late summer patterns, feeding and watering in generally the same areas. But nothing I had done proved successful. I had hunted the only food plot in

The author spent many years conducting helicopters surveys on some of the best whitetail habitat in Texas, during which time he saw several hundred thousands of bucks. However, he only saw three typical 14 pointers during that time. When he finally saw this Texas buck, he hunted him hard, and through persistence finally took him.

Mid-Day Whitetails
Caught on Camera

134

the area, hunted staging areas where the trails leading into the food plots came together, used rattling horns to imitate pre-rut rubbing on trees and minor sparring between bucks. I had even tried baiting, legal in Texas. And, yes, I had seen the buck but he had come in after legal shooting time. So when Rafael told me the buck was feeding and moving primarily after dark, it didn't surprise me, nor that he suggested I hunt during the middle of the day. I asked Rafael what else I could do to take this buck. He simply rolled his eyes and shrugged his shoulders. "Me no say..."

Years ago when I started hunting the famed South Texas Brush Country, I had often chosen one buck seen during our helicopter game survey and hunted him exclusively, win or lose. Doing so, I learned much—which was most of the time the buck came out the winner!

I spent the next four days seeing bucks, does, javelinas, wild hogs, coyotes and bobcats—even found some cougar tracks; pretty well the usual characters encountered on a good South Texas whitetail hunt. But the big 14-point typical continued to evade me. Business required me to leave for a week, which would put me back on the property during full moon.

Driving to the ranch, I recalled one of my first South Texas hunts. An invitation from a rancher brought me there. I arrived at 4 a.m. to be sure we'd be out well before daylight. To my chagrin there were no lights on in the ranch house until about 5. Shortly thereafter I was inside visiting with the rancher and other hunters he had in camp. When the hunters left, the rancher poured another cup of coffee, and we adjourned to his living room. There we talked of hunting other parts of the world, looked at African and Asian trophies on his wall, and looked at volume after volume of hunting photos. All the time I was tremendously anxious to get into the brush. The sun was way above the horizon when I glanced at the clock on his wall: 9 o'clock! "Well they should be coming back shortly, about time for us to leave. Grab your rifle and some rattling horns and we'll head out in about 30 minutes."

I couldn't believe it was 9 o'clock and we still had not yet left camp. Finally, we loaded into his old Jeep. As we headed out of the

"I learned a long time ago, when approaching or at full moon or when there is hardly any moon, and moon position is such that it's overhead around noon or at midnight, whitetails tend to move best during the hours of 10 a.m. till about 3 p.m. Too, to some extent, I think deer have patterned us as hunters and know most hunters are in the field early and late and seldom during midday!"

compound, the other hunters were coming back to camp. "See anything Joe?" questioned the old rancher.

"Naw, just a couple of does and a young buck, nothing worth getting excited about!" came the reply from the hunter.

Before we got more than 200 yards from the house, we talked to three more groups of hunters. All reported seeing only does and young bucks. The rancher told each there was food on the stove and the coffee was hot. "We'll see you about the time you guys start heading out at 3."

By now, it was almost 10 o'clock. We had driven less than a quarter mile from headquarters when we saw our first deer—mature bucks rubbing their antlers, feeding, obviously checking scrapes and making moves on does. Less than a half mile from camp, we rattled up bucks. By the time we headed back to the ranch headquarters just before 3 o'clock we had looked over no less than 32 different bucks. Normally several of those would have fit my bill, but, we were hoping I could take a particular buck my rancher friend had in mind, an 8-point he thought would score in the mid-150s.

As we headed back to camp, the rancher casually mentioned to me, "When we meet the hunters, let me do the talking." We pulled into the compound almost straight up 3 o'clock, and hunters were readying themselves for the afternoon hunt.

"See anything?" queried the hunters.

"No sir! I guess you guys were right. It really is slow out there today. Didn't see a thing worth shooting!" he said as he turned my way and winked, then smiled. I hunted four days with my friend, and we never left camp before 9, or hunted after 3 in the afternoon. When I questioned him about this one evening, he replied, "I learned a long time ago, when approaching or at full moon or when there is hardly any moon, and moon position is such that it's overhead around noon or at midnight, whitetails tend to move best during the hours of 10 a.m. till about 3 p.m. Too, to some extent, I think deer have patterned us as hunters and know most hunters are in the field early and late and seldom during midday!" I took to heart what he said and what I had seen.

In ensuing years I've taken some really great bucks, most of my biggest, during midday.

When I returned to the hunting property where we had been seen the big typical 14-point, it was the day before full moon. I hoped the buck would be active during midday, but I started the day at first light, actually before first light. For the first four hours of the day's hunt, I saw only some does and fawns. I rattled horns numerous times, but nothing showed. Then just before noon, I rattled horns once again and within moments was surrounded by four different bucks—one, a mature 10-point that was absolutely breathtaking! I considered for a moment taking him, but he wasn't the buck I was hunting for, and he looked a bit young. About an hour later I rattled up two more bucks at a different setup.

I decided to set up along a creek bottom on a trail that led to a waterhole. It was nearly 1 p.m. I leaned back against a rough-barked mesquite tree, set my shooting stick in front of me where I rested my Ruger Super Blackhawk Hunter .44 Mag as well as my stalking shield. I didn't have long to wait. I heard and then saw movement coming my way. I could see about a hundred yards, at the end of which was a small opening in the brush and tall grass.

It was the big typical 14-point. He stopped in the opening at the end of my shooting lane and turned broadside. I quickly centered the crosshairs of my .44 Mag on his shoulder, cocked the hammer on the single-action Ruger, and then gently pulled the trigger. The buck simply dropped. I quickly cocked the revolver's hammer again and kept it trained on the downed buck. When there was no movement after about a minute, I headed to where he lay. At my feet lay a typical 14 point, easily grossing over the Boone and Crockett minimum, and he was mine!

Midday hunting has often helped me take great whitetails, but occasionally I have had to resort to other techniques, some of which might be a bit offbeat!

Years ago I met a gentlemen in my hometown who was extremely successful in taking mature bucks. When I initially questioned him about his techniques he simply smiled and wouldn't tell me. It wasn't until several years later and getting to know me better that he told me how he took old, mature bucks with impressive racks. "I make them mad!" he said. I must have had a questioning look on my face. "I make them mad so that they have to return to their scrapes to freshen them more often." Again I must have had a questioning look on my face. "I make them mad by urinating in their scrapes, so they have to come more often to freshen them." He continued, "Before hunting I drink a lot of water! Then whenever I find scrapes, I urinate in each one. Quite often shortly after my doing so, the buck returns... particularly right before the rut really gets going strong. This makes him mad by X-ing out his scrape and he keeps coming back more often." I am not one to argue with success! And obviously my friend had been extremely successful in taking big bucks. Although he had never entered any of his whitetails, I knew he had in his collection of mounts at least four that would easily make book, and another four that were really close to making the All-time list.

I took his technique to heart, or should I say to kidneys. I started doing what he had done in scrapes on a ranch I used more for research than hunting. Nearly each time I urinated in a fairly fresh scrape within less than an hour a buck came to freshen it. Most of the bucks doing so were mature with sizable antlers. Next I started using the technique while hunting on prime property and again, within less than an hour in most instances, a buck appeared and "X-ed out" my scrape activity. I started taking some really nice mature bucks with impressive antlers, this on property where the best bucks scored in the high 140s or so.

The first time I tried it in South Texas, a book buck appeared within less than an hour and X-ed out what I had done. I didn't shoot him because he was only about 4 years old. The property where I hunted held other bucks which had equally impressive antlers and were considerably older. Our game plan on the property was to take only bucks 6 years and older.

On my next trip for whitetails in South Texas, I hunted a ranch that held numerous really good bucks. When I arrived at the ranch, the owner and manager told me hunting had been tough. While some good bucks had been seen, none had been taken. They told me their trail cameras, which I personally do not use because I love the mystery of what I might see, indicated there was a really big typical 11-point that grossed 175 or so that had recently been photographed on the edge of a food plot making a scrape. He was making scrapes was he?

Early next morning I drank several cups of coffee, several glasses of orange juice and four glasses of water. I practically waddled when I walked away from the breakfast table and headed to the food plot where the buck had been seen. In the darkness with the aid of a flashlight I located the scrape the buck had been seen visiting. There I relieved myself, then

The author with a near B&C South Texas whitetail he took after personally "freshening" the buck's scrape for several days..

138

...Again I must have had a questioning look on my face. "I make them mad by urinating in their scrapes, so they have to come more often to freshen them."

139

walked to a big mesquite and set up my stalking shield. At first light two different bucks, albeit younger ones, walked by the scrape to freshen it.

When activity ceased I walked back to the scrape and freshened it myself once again. Then I headed to another area. Throughout the middle part of the day I hunted not far from the food plot and several times walked to the scrape and freshened it, noticing bucks had visited it since I had last been there.

I had planned to hunt all day long but made a quick trip to the lodge to grab a bite to eat and some more things to drink, then hurriedly headed back to the brush to set up on trails leading to the scrape. Each time nature called, I freshened the scrape again, and then sat where I could watch it. Several bucks came by to X-out my activity, but not the one I hunted. As the afternoon sun started sliding into the mesquites to the west, I wondered if the buck I was hunting would show. Others had, but not him.

The sun was all but gone when a buck walked into the food plot just to the east, down wind of the scrape. He raised his head and then immediately walked to the scrape. My crosshairs were on him when he stopped. I gently tugged the trigger of my .30-06 Ruger American rifle. The buck pitched forward and was down. I've successfully used the same oddball technique many times.

Speaking of sense of smell, over the years I tried just about all the no-scent liquids, clothing and other apparatus. None have ever worked to my satisfaction. In doing so, I saw that deer seemed to notice blaze orange. While I'm not certain exactly how they perceive it with their eyes, they obviously see it as something different.

Combining smell and sight, several years ago I started playing games with whitetail deer. As a youngster I learned deer seldom pay too much attention to things they become used to, be it something they see every day and/or something they smell every day. We used to hang sweaty clothes on the barbed wire around our watermelon patch in an effort to keep deer away from the ripening melons. First day they avoided the area, second time we did it, they approached to the smell of the clothing. Third time we did it, they acted if nothing was there and ate our melons!

Taking that experience into account while hunting in Kentucky where blaze orange vests and caps (or head covers) are required, I started hanging blaze orange vest and caps in the ground blinds I hunted from

For those not interested in hunting by waiting in a blind, try a stalking shield.

well before the season opened. I also started hanging sweaty clothes, worn socks, and underwear in those same open ground blinds. Then I started monitoring deer activity by looking at tracks. Same thing happened as it had when I was a kid growing up with hanging clothes to keep deer out of our melon patches; by the fourth day or so of seeing and smelling the new sights and odors, the deer started paying little to no attention to them.

Getting deer used to human odors and even human shape in hunting situations is something I have long done. I've occasionally used mannequins, and set them in natural ground blinds dressed partially in blaze orange. I've used these in numerous states where blaze orange is required. When and where possible I've also asked locals to hang recently worn clothes in the immediate area where I plan to hunt from, changing them out with fresh recent work clothes about every three or so days— more often if possible. Generally I start doing both blaze orange and worn clothes a month before the season opens.

LEFT: The author with a near "book" whitetail taken in northern Missouri after days of hanging blaze orange and "worn socks" in the area where he had previously seen this buck.

ABOVE: An Oklahoma whitetail the author took from a makeshift ground blind where for two weeks before he had placed a blaze orange cap and vest to get local deer used to the sight of the blaze orange.

It's better to accustom whitetails to sights and smells rather than try to find ways to cover or mask such scents and sights.

I used to hunt some extremely good whitetail property in south-central Oklahoma and in western Kentucky. In both instances, I only hunted from natural ground blinds. At least a month before the opening of the hunting season I hung a blaze orange vest and cap where I would be sitting. I also routinely hung worn shirts, socks and underwear in the same ground blind. If I couldn't do it, I had a friend do it for me.

By the time hunting season arrived, the deer had grown completely accustomed to the sight of the blaze orange and the smell of humans in the immediate area where I hunted. When I arrived wearing blaze orange and smelling like a human, both does and bucks paid no attention to my presence. Not only did I do this in my ground blinds but others where guests hunted. They reported the same thing I did: deer paid no attention to their presence. This helped us and particularly me to take some extremely good and interesting mature bucks, including several near B&C minimums! These were bucks which, had I not gotten them accustomed to the smell of humans and the sight of blaze orange where I hunted, I might never have seen.

To me, it's better to accustom whitetails to sights and smells rather than try to find ways to cover or mask such scents and sights.

When it comes to hunting and taking mature whitetails, dare to hunt when and where others do not, dare to hunt all day long and don't ever look for excuses not to go hunting. Dare too, to be different and to try different techniques, even sometime those which seem to go against what others have taught you. Think!

Weishuhn with his 127-4/8 B&C record book non-typical Coues' whitetail deer taken in Sonora, Mexico. The buck was taken during mid-day while other hunters were in camp having lunch and resting....

The Elusive Whitetail in Texas
René R. Barrientos | Managing and Hunting Private Land

LUCK ALONE CAN BE THE FACTOR IN HARVESTING THE WHITE-
tail trophy of a lifetime, but to put oneself in a position to consistently hunt trophy whitetail requires more than luck. It requires patience,
planning and hard work.

My hunting goal for decades was to find and harvest one buck that
would make the Boone and Crockett records book. I reached that goal in
2003. As of 2013, I have now taken 10 All-time B&C whitetails. In 1996,
I purchased an 8,000-acre ranch in La Salle County, Texas, with strong
soils where we have implemented a wildlife management program that
in 10 seasons has resulted in this property yielding 14 "book" deer—11
typical bucks netting over 170 and three non-typicals netting over 195. This
calculates an average of one book deer per 571 acres over a 10-year period.
To put this harvest yield into perspective, to have an equivalent production,
calculate the property one has access to via ownership or lease and divide
by 571 and you can evaluate rates of productivity. However, there are many
ranches in this eco-region with better soils which are also producing very
large deer—or at least have the potential to do so.

This success can be attributed to a combination of conservation and
habitat strategies that we have implemented through our ranch management
plan, which emphasizes how habitat plays a large part in the scheme. I'll
talk about the reasons for each aspect of our plan, including our harvest
criteria for all age groups; scouting that allows us to make hunting and
harvesting decisions for the current and future seasons; efforts that have
allowed us to consistently harvest many large deer—some which made the
Boone and Crockett records book; a non-pedantic discussion on gear and
hunting; and our philosophy on hunter management, the most difficult
element in implementing a long-term plan that is often overlooked, usually
causing many well-intentioned programs to falter. These opinions are by no
means definitive, but rather, anecdotal.

Range conditions in this last decade of extreme weather conditions, be it unprecedented drought or the occasional rainy year, can have a detrimental effect on a whitetail deer's ability to express their antler growth potential. However sound the carefully planned management, marginal range conditions can be a major factor influencing whitetail deer. Native habitat is the cornerstone of our management program. By deliberately enhancing this native habitat and implementing several management practices, we have created a condition to hunt and harvest large, mature, native, free-ranging whitetail bucks season after season, regardless of drought or marginal range conditions in a fair-chase scenario. The program has effectively neutralized the otherwise potentially devastating effects of extreme weather conditions in South Texas.

The basic premise to our conservation strategy is:

1) Have a plan to implement that is based on preserving native habitat;

2) Control the deer population to avoid exceeding the carrying capacity of the native habitat;

3) Maintain balanced sex ratios and age structure within the deer herd;

4) Have water sources readily available for all wildlife species and;

5) Minimize any mechanical disturbance or damage to the native plant community.

We have had the same management/conservation plan for 17 years, under the assistance of biologists Jimmy Rutledge and now Alan Cain of the Texas Parks and Wildlife Department (TPWD), with only minor adjustments, which entailed modifying the harvest criteria based on score as our goals were met.

There is a misconception that the more deer you carry on a given property the greater the odds of having more large-antlered whitetail deer. I feel this assumption is mistaken; by doing so, a manager may actually detrimentally affect the health and antler growth of the deer and may eventually damage the native plant community. Our recipe is simple: the less deer, the bigger the bucks and does, assuming the number of deer is balanced to the available habitat. Having a harvest criteria that allows the larger-antlered bucks to grow older and benefit from greater available

The forbs and woody plants in South Texas are what deer thrive on and should never be sacrificed for or replaced with food plots. Nature does a swell job.

nutrition immensely helps the remaining does and fawns as well. Of equal—if not more—importance is that a management plan should always assume a drought year, that is, manage for the worst range conditions rather than optimum ones when calculating carrying capacity.

You need to know the soils and habitat on your hunting property, and your management plan has to be based on consistency and patience. One thing that I cannot emphasize enough is that one should never trade a single acre of native habitat for an acre of food plots as the habitat will provide much-needed poundage of feed for deer and all wildlife in dry years and require no labor or money to maintain, while food plots may provide little or no nutritional value or shade when animals may need it the most. If not irrigated, these plots produce nothing in dry years. According to Val Lehmann, an early Texas pioneer in wildlife management, "although brush may be brush to the casual observer, woody plants vary greatly in quality and value to both game and livestock."

Whitetail deer in South Texas prefer forbs. They browse on woody plants and cactus, which provide incredible and varying amounts of protein during different periods of the year that are especially beneficial under dry conditions. In dry years, the mesquite tree blooms can yield up to three fruit or bean crops annually; the bean crop production turns off in wet years and is the period when these trees have their greatest growth. (Nature does a pretty good job in spite of us at times!) This is evident when some of South Texas' biggest bucks are harvested in dry years. Why? Some of the most palatable and preferred plants available have protein levels that increase in the hot summer months in contrast to most other shrubs or woody plants that have declining protein levels. As a result, deer have great protein forage from such plants as the mesquite (up to 16 percent protein value), cactus (up to 10 percent protein), guayacan (up to 23 percent) and granjeno (up to 25 percent). Cactus itself can be a critical reserve of green forage for animals in severe drought years. While the cactus has lower protein levels, its sugar content is a great energy source, and when combined with the protein yield from mesquite beans during these dry periods, it exemplifies the evolution of our habitat that benefits much of our diverse native wildlife populations. The yield from a single acre of good strong habitat in an average year is 1,400 pounds per year in forbs and leaves from woody plants alone, along with their fruit such as mesquite beans, huisachillo seed and cactus pear can yield an additional 3,000 pounds. The overall crude protein from this

The delivery vehicle for cottonseed is a 6-foot-length of horse V-mesh wire tied in a cylinder shape, placed loosely with a T-post in the center to hold it upright. Having any type of supplemental feed to assist wildlife is just that, a seasonal supplement and not a substitute for native habitat.

native habitat ranges from 6 to 25 percent. Northern states do have higher biomass, but the habitat in South Texas has a higher nutrition concentration. This nutritional yield would be absent from a food plot that sacrificed this valuable food source otherwise available year-round.

I initially made the mistake of thinking food plots would add value to our habitat strategy. And although they can be useful as a hunting tool, they should not be used to replace natural habitat. These plots require time and expense to maintain and return minimal benefit, especially with nature having to take decades to recover from the removal of good habitat acreage.

A good source to help in identifying South Texas habitat and its intricacies is *A Field Guide to Common South Texas Shrubs* (1977) by Richard Taylor, Jimmy Rutledge and Joe Herrera, all (now retired) Texas Parks and Wildlife Department (TPWD) biologists formerly assigned to South Texas. It is a very accessible manual to help identify most native brush, their nutritional crude protein value in different times of the year, and utilization by wildlife. If referenced, one will realize and appreciate how important the available brush is, its role, and how best to utilize it in helping grow big deer—and consequently, benefit all other native wildlife.

Having supplemental feed to assist wildlife is just that, a supplement and not a substitute for deer habitat. I was very fortunate to have as a neighbor and friend, William "Bill" A. Maltsberger, whom I consider the most knowledgeable person on ranching, deer and livestock in South Texas. He has studied the diets and behavior of deer as well as the benefits of incorporating cattle in the equation of wildlife since they have a symbiotic relationship that can be mutually beneficial. Many of the finest wildlife biologists have gone to him for his opinions as he is much more than just a casual observer of this incredible species and I followed his suggestions and example in our plan. In addition, I was assigned Jaime "Jimmy" Rutledge, a very talented biologist from the TPWD who assisted us in formulating a long-term wildlife management plan to benefit all native wildlife species. Seventeen years ago, as we began to conserve our native plant species to benefit wildlife, we heeded their suggestion and began putting out whole cottonseed as a supplement, making sure that it was dairy quality and aflatoxin-tested. The does were helped immensely during their periods of pre-fawning, fawning, and lactation, resulting in bigger offspring. We were targeting does primarily, since we wanted bigger and healthier fawns to carry forward in future years. It is a seasonal supplement that we use also to help post-rut bucks regain their weight lost (40-45 pounds) during the rut. Their better health condition results in a later period of shedding of their antlers and regrowth for the coming season. We have a higher fawn survival than most ranches, so the bad rap of the effects of Gossypol in cottonseed causing infertility is misplaced; the low consumption rate as a supplement is of no negative consequence in our experience. The upside is that the delivery vehicle for cottonseed we have in the pasture is a relatively low cost (about $7.00); it is a 6-foot-length of horse V-mesh wire tied in a cylinder shape, placed loosely with a T-post in the center to hold it upright. Supplementation is not a substitute for native habitat and is never a rationale for exceeding the carrying capacity of your property.

The most crucial periods to supplement bucks can be narrowed down to two. January through March is a time period where one can optimize post-rut shape of the bucks since the range is in tough winter mode. The second is July 1 through the end of August, which coincides with the

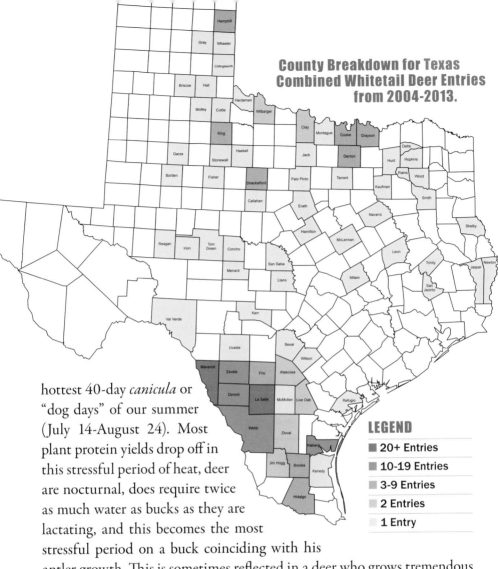

LEGEND

- 20+ Entries
- 10-19 Entries
- 3-9 Entries
- 2 Entries
- 1 Entry

hottest 40-day *canicula* or "dog days" of our summer (July 14-August 24). Most plant protein yields drop off in this stressful period of heat, deer are nocturnal, does require twice as much water as bucks as they are lactating, and this becomes the most stressful period on a buck coinciding with his antler growth. This is sometimes reflected in a deer who grows tremendous G-1s, 2s, and 3s, but has unimpressive short G-4s—a symptom of reduced nutrition combined with range condition stress from summer heat.

The Boone and Crockett Club records allow us to isolate certain areas in each state that have produced records-book deer over the years, and for the most part I feel the trophy qualities can be attributed to the soils, range, and habitat present in these areas. Put in simpler terms, if you want to harvest big deer, then go where you can expect to find them. There are outliers but they are usually the exception rather than the rule. I used this information to decide where to invest my time and efforts to make a difference in conservation and hunting satisfaction (See B&C Texas Map). The soil types and water availability are crucial. The conscious decision of developing a long-term management program requires not only taking the proper steps, but having an understanding and appreciation of why you are doing these things.

In Texas we are fortunate to have the Texas Parks and Wildlife Department and its personnel who provide landowners and lessees all the tools via advice and permits to assist in developing a management plan, assist in determining the population and suggest an optimum harvest to sustain the carrying capacity by evaluating the utilization of the habitat. A word of caution based on observation: be wary of a few of the private-contract biologists (many I refer to as promoters as this is a form of the commercialization of wildlife) who are readily available to provide their friends with work by bulldozing your native habitat to build food plots, provide the required equipment or contractors to maintain these plots, provide their unique seed source and supply you with special supplemental feed. They will also "assist" you in hunting your deer, conduct outfitting on your property, provide unneeded construction, find "imported" genetics to supposedly get around a long-term program, etc., with a hidden contractor percentage fee on top of their bill. The consequence will be an eventual unnecessary financial reduction of your funds keyed on your enthusiasm to develop a plan which will result in being short-sighted and disappointing. So when they extend their hand to shake yours, be sure to hold on to your wallet with your free hand as they will help themselves if you let them. That being said, there are many honest, talented and credible private-contract biologists that can provide you with good, strong, proven direction as most properties require very little, other than developing water, a reduction in numbers, shift in age groups in the deer population, and a harvest criteria to allow those few promising bucks to mature and reach their greatest potential.

There are numerous sources of credible and reliable deer research literature such as those available online from the Caesar Kleberg Wildlife Research Institute at Texas A&M University–Kingsville and the Quality Deer Management Association. Others may not be as reliable.

I enjoy and have learned much from reading these articles, but I remain at times skeptical of conclusions reached as the critical eye of the landowner/lessee hunter can observe differences or contradictions depending on the particular circumstances or variations. One general research conclusion that I disagree with is that culling (or a targeted harvest) has no effect on a deer herd. While scrutinizing the research I find our observations contradict their findings. I attribute this discrepancy to the size of the study area, minimal or inconsequential harvest numbers, and populations used. As the control sites proximity allowed natural migration between the two and skewed the results. One does not change the genetics of whitetail deer, but one can influence a change in the offspring of the bucks not harvested at too young an age by allowing them to live long enough to take advantage of the native habitat. An approach is removing bucks with some trait that you consider undesirable, whether it is short beam length, length of tines, number of tines, body size, etc. Our harvest criteria and its results over long periods of time have influenced our deer and will be discussed further below.

There are two very good recent literature sources that one should read to be able to evaluate scientific conclusions to base decisions on science but be reserved with respect to the expressed and espoused conclusions. One is, "Disinterested Science, the Basis of our Roosevelt Doctrine," by Valerius Geist, Ph.D., in the Winter 2013 issue of *Fair Chase* magazine, that discusses there being "no shortage of advocacy masquerading as science, as well as lamentable flaws inflicted by scientists themselves...". Geist's knowledge, analysis and voice is unparalleled in the field of wildlife and conservation. This should be read in conjunction with the article by Steve Nelle, called "Lessons from Leopold, Professors and Poets" in the November 2013 issue of *Texas Wildlife* magazine, wherein he discusses that land and wildlife managers "must base their action and plans on the best science available, but they must also be able to perceive what science is not able to explain," as this is what land stewardship represents.

Managing water is a crucial aspect of a land management plan for maintaining healthy deer populations as South Texas does not have an abundance of water. Our long-term plan included expanding water sites available for wildlife and livestock with realistic annual distribution expansions. Water is good for all wildlife—from insects for quail and turkeys to lactating does during the hot summer months. A mistake I made early on—at a significant construction cost—regarding water sites, which I promptly corrected, was an attempt to use large concrete troughs designed for cattle. Due to the high evaporation rates, especially in summer heat, if there is not high usage and water turnover by livestock, the water quality diminishes to the point where deer do not utilize the troughs and require constant monitoring. The alternative we found to be ideal for South Texas summers, where evaporation can be up to 6 feet—and assuming water is available via waterlines to replenish the evaporation—is an earthen waterhole where the bacteria in the soil maintains the quality of the water. My preferred dimensions are 60 x90 and 8- to 10-feet deep, which can be dug in one day by a D-6 dozer at a minimal cost. In creating these earthen waterholes, the earth is removed and distanced away from the edge to limit erosion back into the water hole. Plus this type of water hole only requires maintenance every four to six years compared to the continued labor needed in keeping the concrete troughs clean. We have had water available for our deer at a rate of one source per 125 acres for about the last 10 years, which coincides with our harvest and management success. Having animals that do not have to travel far for water distributes them well and minimizes the role that dominance plays. Concentrating animals because of limited water sources can result in a degradation of the native habitat in the vicinity of the water, as well as concentrating predators—contrary to the management and conservation one is seeking to achieve for all wildlife.

HARVEST CRITERIA

The most economical and best tool available to any individual to manage their property for trophy whitetail is a bullet. The carrying capacity of an individual property is based on the soil types and available native habitat, regardless of supplementation—crucial for maintaining ideal body weight and body condition of deer. Carrying capacity determines the conditions for selective harvesting of does and bucks in all age groups to maximize the goals set by the management plan. Harvesting is a matter of removing a set number of deer, and that number should not be compromised once the appropriate goal is set.

Before I acquired this ranch, the only management present could better be described as mismanagement. Simply put, it was great in soils but had a harvest policy of "top-shooting," which was to shoot the biggest bucks regardless of age class, leave the less desirable bucks, and ignore the doe population. The initial census showed one deer for every six acres (a vast overpopulation) a doe-to-buck ratio that was skewed, minimal water availability easily affected by drought, and a top-heavy population of mature bucks that no one would want to shoot. The only promising deer were the young deer.

The TPWD biologist, Jimmy Rutledge, had a daunting task, but once a five-year goal was set, his advice amounted to a lot of work, primarily removing large numbers of does and mature bucks. To get a handle on the reproduction, we decided to harvest as many does as possible, preferably older does, with the goal of one doe per buck ratio. We also removed all spikes and all mature bucks with eight points or less and any with low scores. We reached our goals after two seasons, and our harvest criteria has been modified over the years to include what we want to allow to mature as part of a balanced, sustainable deer population with increases in body weights and antler expression. We feel a buck-to-doe ratio of 1-to-1 works and allows us to keep up with reproductive rates. A balanced age structure in bucks is simple: one-third young (age 1-½ to 2-½), one-third middle age (3-½ to 4-½), and one-third mature (age 5-½-plus) so that as deer are harvested and removed there is always an upcoming buck to replace the harvested older deer.

DOES

Our annual doe harvest criteria is to select a number of does to remove based on the estimated fawn crop by 110 percent, assuming 50 percent of the fawns are does. We err on the side of removal and prefer removing the older does that are easier to identify by the head shape and ears as well as all does that have twin fawns since a single fawn will always be bigger and healthier than a twin. There are a couple of studies that opine that older does tend to have a disproportionate number of doe fawns versus buck fawns. Based on our field observations over several years, we feel we had a higher number of buck fawns than doe fawns, which if correct, was an unintended benefit to our doe harvest criteria. The doe harvest is allotted by pasture or area within a pasture to not over-remove does from a particular area as some areas are easier to hunt than others and they tend to remain in the area where they were born. Good nutrition at an early age makes a buck and doe a bigger-framed deer. We do not harvest does until after the rut—to allow the fawns to be weaned by the mother rather than by harvest. The timing also allows fawns to acquire better survival skills and lessen winter mortality. We see much bigger and heavier fawns in December at the start of the rut as they have had a head start over those whose mothers were removed in October or November on other ranches. As a result, it is not uncommon to have mature does weighing 140-160 pounds when you combine a later doe harvest in January and February with maturity and lower deer densities commensurate to a particular property.

RANCH HARVEST GUIDELINES BY AGE

These are our current guidelines that can be modified for different populations depending on herd condition, antler size to a particular property, and management stage.

YEARLINGS AND SPIKES
Remove all spikes.

Hopefully all are yearlings, and if not, then you have a harvest problem. A few biologists claim that they have found a very rare spike that may grow into a 150-inch-class deer at maturity, but our expectations are much higher than a mature 150-inch buck, and we have ample hunting opportunities under our criteria to not have a spike reproduce or take the place of a 10-point yearling. The Kerr Wildlife Management Area studies of spikes are definitive in this area as far as I am concerned. Because of drought conditions, we have allowed forked yearlings to have another year to show what they might become, subject to the number we have targeted as necessary to maintain our numbers.

2-½ YEAR OLDS
Remove all bucks that have no brows.

3-½ YEAR OLDS
Remove all bucks that have less than eight points, unless they are with three or four bucks in the same age group who are short-tined or more than eight points, then use discretion to remove that deer.

4-½ YEAR OLDS
Remove all eight-point frame deer or less, regardless of any additional abnormal points; remove all bucks that have short beams or short G-1s regardless of number of points.

5-½ YEAR OLDS
Remove all nine-point frame deer or less and any buck scoring less than 150-inches, regardless of the number of points.

6-½ YEAR OLDS
Remove all bucks that are less than 155 inches and include the above criteria as well.

7-½ YEAR OLDS & OLDER
Include the above criteria. Harvest your trophies, and only exclude those bucks considered for being carried to the next season.

Refer to Chapter 4 on page 74 for complete details on techniques for aging bucks on the hoof.

This 6x7 was seen only once in the prior season and once during pre-season scouting for a few seconds. I realized the only plan available due to extremely heavy brush was to hunt him at 175 yards where he'd previously crossed a sendero. It took 8 days of hunting before he showed himself.

BUCKS

Relating our current buck harvest criteria can be complicated, but in the end it is guided by the consideration as to whether we want a particular buck over a different buck of that age group to breed and be allowed an opportunity for further growth. We initially began harvesting trophies when the deer reached age 7-½, then reduced the prime trophy harvest age to 6-½. But we saw that at 5-½, most of these bucks, at their prime age, were so worn down by the rut that they had the most weight to regain post-rut compared to older deer. We were disappointed that some 5-½ year olds had little increase in score attributable to the consequence of a hard rut. We feel that a 6-½-year-old buck can recover quicker and its body condition lends itself to having a higher probability of significant antler growth in following year. This was confirmed by many of the 5-½-year-old bucks not having the 10 percent-plus jump in antler size we were hoping for. We believe that as long as the mature deer's teeth are in good shape and not

We deliberately chose to not harvest a particular buck in 2003 that we estimated to be 6-½ with double-row points. I harvested this non-typical in 2009 with a final B&C net score of 219-3/8 and a B&C gross score of 224-2/8 points. It has similar antler formations to that 2003 buck we let go and never hunted.

showing any more wear than a 5-½ year old, that the 6-½-year-old bucks should continue in their prime for several more years—through 8-½ and possibly 9-½. An additional indicator, comparing the beam length of sheds from the same deer, has shown a measurable length or distance from the burr to the base of the G-1 as deer are allowed to age. Many can continue to lengthen their beams, assuming a stable nutritional plane, and one can start to see 26 to 29-inch-plus beams. Other outstanding ranches in South Texas that continually harvest monster whitetails do so at 7-½ to 8-½ years of age by design. The same age assumption cannot be made for northern deer, where harsh winters can result in shorter life spans and different nutritional stress than deer in Texas. However, based on our observations and experience on the ground, we strive to harvest our trophies at age 7-½, regardless of their antler size at 5-½ or 6-½.

Older bucks are not as aggressive; they are larger and heavier, less active and more nocturnal, only showing at the peak of the rut rather than the pre-rut stages, making them more challenging to locate and hunt. Their maturity and acquired experience over the years allows many of them to survive all our hunting efforts to locate and harvest them, so it must be enjoyed and appreciated that they gave us great hunting opportunities. When successful, the joy is tempered with the knowledge that this particular fine specimen who conquered years of survival is gone, and the excitement and anticipation of looking for him and observing him in the wild is over.

We expect to yield long-term dividends by making the conscious decision to not top-shoot all the better-scoring bucks, so we choose to carry over a few of them each year to see whether they could or would continue to grow, even if at smaller increments, or to not harvest them altogether. I believe that if there is an antler trait that is of particular interest to the person formulating their management plan—be it split G-2s, double row of tines, particularly long beams or tines, etc.—one should try to avoid the temptation of removing that buck. We deliberately chose to never harvest a particular buck in 2003 that we estimated to be 6-½ and pushing 190 inches with double-row points, and in the ensuing years we have seen many bucks, even 10 years later, that are quite similar in unique antler formation. One non-typical harvested in 2009 gross-scored 224-2/8 and netted 219-3/8.

SCOUTING

To be able to get a grasp on the deer population, antler growth from the prior years' seasons, and to better age bucks to make a determination as to whether they are ready for harvesting, there is nothing more important than days in the field. Three products are worthwhile for helping accomplish this: the field and/or video camera, the Thermacell bug repellent device, and improved scope reticles for hunting, such as the B&C Big Game Reticle offered by Leupold.

Our scouting actually begins in April and May by finding the occasional shed and recording its location. A particular outstanding shed, whether an unknown or recognizable buck, allows one to make a calculation of a buck and is a good indicator of where this buck may be found pre-rut. In 2003, I had never seen the first book deer that I harvested (182-1/8 net), but I had found its shed—with a mass measurement in excess of 40 inches—approximately 400 yards from where I eventually hunted him based on the shed location. We had just begun using field cameras with

35mm film—so we were quite limited as to the number of photos taken. He had never showed up in any photos. Finding a particular shed also gives one an idea of an area to target for physical scouting near water early in the pre-season as most deer are nocturnal in the heat, and you are limited to 15-20 minutes of movement. That is why we target water since deer have poor radiators and prefer to drink in the shadows at or after sunset.

In addition to sitting near water for scouting, if we have a long *sendero* (road) that is 500 yards to a mile in length, we will sit with a spotting scope. If we see any deer that appear interesting, we later cut the distance down to a few hundred yards based on landmarks. We do not like to crowd a buck as a 6-½ to 7-½-year-old buck is difficult enough to hunt without him knowing he is being hunted and turn nocturnal, as they often do. Once a good observation along with some video or photo is obtained, it is best to back off, leave that deer alone, and have him as comfortable in his area without any added pressure.

Aside from finding sheds in spring, our field scouting begins in August while the deer are in the later stages of antler growth, although 20 percent of our mature bucks are still in velvet in early October. I attribute the later shedding and antler growing periods as a sign of good body condition coming out of the winter and rut. This seems to coincide with mosquitoes as well as white biting gnats which always seem to be present! I was a skeptic when a few of my friends would carry a Thermacell with them. However, once I tried it, I was sold on its ability to deter swarms of these insects and making a hot session of sitting in the shade next to a waterhole or pond more tolerable during scouting (but not used during serious hunting).

We combine our sitting and field observations with placing cameras for five-day increments and concentrate on a single area to get as many deer as possible on film—fully understanding that a large number of bucks will not be found by cameras, and no area should be ignored. Field scouting is more effective, but cameras do allow one to cover a larger area, and on occasion, locate a deer that can then be targeted for physical scouting. Devote time to aging and field scoring so a decision can be made, video taken with location and time recorded for later reference.

We are only able to make a decision to actually hunt a particular buck once we estimate his age and whether we want to dedicate our time hunting that particular deer over another. There is difficulty in aging and field scoring a buck as the body size of a particular buck plays a huge factor in reaching an estimated score: A big, heavy bodied buck in the 260-pound-plus weight range with a large set of antlers versus a smaller-framed buck weighing 210 pounds with the same antlers makes the smaller animal appear to be 10 to 20 percent larger. One indicator we advise to look at is the length of the neck and front legs as smaller-framed deer are shorter, and it is best noticed when there are other bucks in the vicinity. I attribute the smaller frame to nutrition, and target these pony deer to be harvested at an earlier age—something we have been doing for all these years, and they have become the exception, now rarely seen on the ranch. However, we are prone to regularly misjudge antler measurements on the hoof based on body size, but hopefully the misjudgment is under-judging.

HUNTING OR CLOSING THE DEAL

Proficiency in shooting falls under the purview of admirable hunting ethics. Although I enjoy long-range shooting, shooting is all it is; it is not hunting, and the game is not part of the sport or challenge of this type of shooting as game cannot be aged or scored at extreme distances. An accurate rifle synchronized for long distances does not make one a hunter.

My opinions here are based on rifle hunting only and not a reflection of my opinion that it is not possible to intensely manage a property with a bow when one has to remove 100 to 300 deer or more because of time and distance constraints, although bowhunting is an immensely challenging hunting experience.

WEAPON

There is no better combination than a bolt-action rifle with good optics that has been sighted in with a specific bullet. There is a trend to use the biggest-objective, highest-magnification rifle scope available with commensurate bells and whistles and the biggest caliber available, both of which are unnecessary in shooting accurately. Although there are several outstanding rifle manufacturers, my preference is a Remington Arms Model 700 VLS in 7mm-08 caliber with a Leupold Vari-X III 3.5-10x40mm objective riflescope, a German-modified post reticle which I have used for at least the last 12 years. This combo has taken all of my book deer to date. I previously hunted with a .25 caliber rifle but changed as I found that a bullet in the 140- to 150-grain range is optimal for a large deer. Most of the time the bullet is found lodged in the opposite side of the shoulder or neck on large bucks, meaning that all the energy was expended on that animal and not a foot-pound of energy is wasted by an exit wound. I hunt deer exclusively with a 140-grain Remington Core-Lokt bullet for deer. This is a great all-around bullet for expansion and repeated accuracy since part of the ethics of hunting demands a quick dispatch of the quarry. After all, on rifle caliber selection, the .270 Winchester served Jack O'Connor well and continues to be a great hunting caliber along with several other tried and proven calibers.

My preference for all our hunters is to not take any shots further than 250 yards as this is the distance where one can generally make a valid decision on age, score, and whether any tines are broken or not. We sight in our rifles at 1-½ inches at 100 yards (which is zero at 200 yards) so that any shot within 250 yards requires no estimations or calculations, minimizes bad shot placement, and as a result we have less than a 1 percent animal loss per season due to a bad shot. An important detail, never rest your rifle stock on a hard surface as the shot will always be slightly higher and to the right if right-handed, so use a glove, cap or pocket-size sandbag (3x2 inches) for accuracy comparable to bench shooting.

We require all of our hunters to sight in their rifles before hunting and have found that about half of these rifles are not accurate due to scope-mounting issues or loose bolts that secure the action to the stock. I cannot explain how or why, but these bolts often become loose. I routinely check my rifle every two weeks for accuracy and screw tightness to minimize any potential problems that can arise. I also suggest hunters purchase all the ammo they might use or need over a season at one time so the ammunition comes from the same manufacturing lot (loaded at the same time). This can instill the confidence of the hunter and result in a successful harvest if the opportunity presents itself.

I would be remiss if I did not mention that we do not allow any single-shot rifle other than a Ruger No. 1 on the ranch even though they are heavily promoted, as there is no comparison to a bolt-action rifle for accuracy. Because our brush is so dense, we like to minimize the wounding and resulting trailing of deer because of an inaccurate shot. In addition, since we prefer shots directly in the center of the shoulder to disable one or both shoulders in trophy deer or at the base of the neck, we do not allow ballistic tips on any bullet as we have seen premature expansion with little or no penetration into the chest cavity resulting in a wound that may not be mortal.

BRIEF TIPS ON GEAR AND HUNTING

When reviewing vintage hunting photos of all the great trophies of years past, whether whitetail or mule deer, grizzly, elk, sheep, pronghorn, moose, or caribou, one missing and obviously unnecessary item was camouflage; hunting skill, patience, and some luck were all that was required. It is no different today.

One cannot control the weather, drought, rains, or wind but must hunt around them and use them to an advantage. The only things needed to hunt whitetail deer, including really big deer, are: patience and willingness to scout and hunt hard; an accurate bolt-action rifle with suitable ammunition and rifle scope; good 10x binoculars; a sharp knife; a flashlight, whether hunting in the morning or evening; clean, quiet clothes; hearing protection; and hunting downwind. That's all.

What you do not need: facial makeup or war paint; camouflage clothing (unnecessary for rifle hunting); scent-cover sprays; carbon-based odor-absorbing outfits; rattling horns, whether real or synthetic; grunt calls, wheezing devices, or whistles; ATVs or specialized vehicles; electric ozone devices; unscented chewing gum; rubber boots; face nets; hearing enhancers, or virtually all other products hawked on media. I am not condemning them, but they are not necessary to "close the deal" as the more gadgets you have, the greater the chance for a mistake. There is nothing wrong with camouflage clothing, but the best available for sturdiness and comfort that are field-proven are military issue.

WIND DIRECTION AND HUNTING LOCATIONS

In South Texas, the prevailing winds are southeasterly in hot or warm weather and northwesterly in cool weather, so one should always set up in the anticipated hunting area depending on wind direction. Hunt downwind, and you eliminate your quarry's keen sense of smell as a defensive mechanism. When setting up a ground position, blind, or tripod, do not put them in the best observation location but rather based on anticipated wind direction. Also take advantage of any available water. Just as importantly, have an entrance and exit plan to not traverse the area you are hunting since you will be alerting animals in the vicinity of your location when getting there early or leaving. Old, mature bucks and does are smarter and much more difficult to hunt as they have gained the hunted experience across the earlier seasons. I mention does because they usually

The most difficult factor is hunter management. The discipline or enforcement of the program rules require that all participants in the hunting process must understand the plan's goals and buy into them. This buck was harvested in 2013.

arrive first and can alert all other deer in the vicinity of your presence. Likewise, avoid being silhouetted—it is simple and easy to sit or place your hunting location in front of or behind brush and sit in the shade if the sun is directly in your face. Additionally, I never use a grunt or call of any kind as you are alerting your prey of your location and hurrying your shot. It is best if your target is unaware of your presence and less alert.

If you have a say or choice in when you hunt, I recommend before the rut as bucks are easier to locate and have not left their range in pursuit of does; and preferably not during a full-moon period. There is no getting around that during the period of a full moon, deer can and do feed all night; therefore, the actual sighting and hunting hours are greatly diminished to a brief period in the morning and at sunset as well as midday from 11:00 a.m. through 2:00 p.m. So get there early and stay as late as possible, though do not ignore hunting in the middle of the day.

Horn rattling during the rut is a lot of fun, but not a good choice because there is insufficient time to make a decision on the age of a trophy, antler identification, field scoring or to judge if a buck has any broken tines—you only have seconds to react. The increased likelihood of making a bad shot also plays into the equation, which is unfair to game. An old buck that has a doe in estrus is unlikely to come to horns, and I would venture to say that most deer shot during a rattling session are young and suffer severe ground shrinkage.

HUNTER MANAGEMENT, THE OVERLOOKED FACTOR

You can have a very well-defined program, easily get the deer to follow the rules and grow old, but the most difficult factor in this equation is the hunter.

From my perspective, the discipline or enforcement of the program rules require that all participants in the hunting process must understand the plan's goals and buy into them. Much of the credit of our management success can be attributed to the friends, workers, and hunters which have understood the consistent benefits of the "program" without whom it would be more difficult. One of my hunting friends, Tommy Baine from Mississippi, an avid deer hunter who has hunted in many states and Canada, says that over the past 30 years he has seen so many deer programs fail because they did not have one strong voice to enforce the rules. He correctly maintains that what is needed is not a deer program but a deer hunter program. Letting deer grow old and not harvesting all the big deer are the two things that, for him, separate good places from great places. You cannot have a democracy in a hunting program that shifts on whims or the latest trends, as this will always gravitate towards mediocrity.

How can a property that provides hunts where everyone that enters the gate is looking to take something from the ranch ever reach its full potential? Participants can have good intentions but mistakes in aging and judging have long-term detrimental effects when one considers how many young bucks are going to be scrutinized and sifted by a harvest criteria over many years to replace that very nice 5-½-year-old deer that had the potential to be a great deer but was removed prematurely. This requires striving for a minimal error tolerance.

Give the land all it needs, give the deer all they need, have a long-term plan, patience and discipline in enforcing the expectations of the program from your hunters. Sounds simple, but it is very hard to do and execute consistently over time.

The final aspect of the hunter program that should not be neglected is that it should be a pleasure to share the fair chase hunting and outdoor experience with friends whose participation is appreciated, and it should never stop being fun. Management is hard work, which has its rewards.

Whitetails North of the Border
Ken Hayworth | Public Land Success

WANT TO BE A TROPHY WHITETAIL HUNTER? YOU HAVE TO GO where the bucks are—not wait for them to come to you. It may be in very large blocks of forest, forest fringe, some level of swamp, or very small tracts of forest in farm land. All areas differ in the most successful ways to hunt, but the same things have to be taken into consideration for each of them. The scent you give off or leave behind, the sound you make, and if you are seen or not all must be addressed in order to be successful in the harvest of a trophy buck.

I have constantly evolved my hunting techniques and strategies and have been fortunate enough to have harvested some very good mature trophy whitetails over the years. Those techniques helped me be successful, and, hopefully they can give you the upper hand on that big buck next year.

Scent, sound, and sight are three things I take into consideration anytime I am in the woods hunting or scouting. Deer have a definite advantage over us in their ability to use these senses to their advantage— something we always have to be aware of when hitting the woods to pursue trophy whitetail. In addition to the above-mentioned concerns, patience is an attribute required of the trophy whitetail hunter. Several of the whitetails I have harvested took me three years before it all came together for a shot. And, each of the trophy deer I have hunted has lived in different types of habitats. I am very fortunate to live in northeastern Saskatchewan and have access to tens of thousands of acres to hunt. The majority of trophy bucks I have taken were hunted on public land, though I never get pinned down to a single area, opting to cover as much territory as I can.

The author with a public-land buck from Saskatchewan. He has constantly evolved his hunting techniques and strategies over the years, taking what he learns from season to season to improve future successes.

8/13/12 9:03 AM

Cuddeback

ABOVE: Set trail cameras in the same location you would later want to hang a treestand or set up a ground blind.

OPPOSITE: Once you have an idea where and when the buck is traveling, use Google Earth to find landmarks and openings in the forest before going in so you have an idea of how far to go and where bedding areas will most likely be. This is a view from one of my treestands.

I start my scouting in early summer spotting from afar, so a good pair of optics is essential. I have a set of 10x56 Swarovski binoculars, but I prefer to utilize my 10x40s. I focus my search on feeding areas this time of year as the deer are very easy to pattern and consistent in their travel routes. I note what time they are moving in the morning and evening, where they come out from cover, and where they go in to cover. I also pay attention to what direction the wind is blowing as I make these observations; movement time and placement will change with winds from varying directions. While scouting, I also try to go unnoticed in my vehicle even if more than a half-mile away.

Once I start finding some bucks that are worth additional effort, I refer to Google Earth maps. This is an awesome tool for finding the type of cover the deer are coming from, such as ridges, swamps, or big timber—very useful in trying to figure out a buck's travel and bedding areas.

Once I have a good idea of the travel habits, I will work my way in closer, usually to within a couple hundred yards from the feeding area, always keeping wind direction in mind. I go out an hour before the regular travel times and will not leave until after dark. I find that after dark the deer are not as likely to be alarmed if they detect movement at a distance.

The author with a wall of extremely impressive whitetail bucks he's harvested over the years. The deer second from the right on the bottom row scores 207 B&C points and was taken during the 2004 season in Saskatchewan.

Set up your blind (top photo shows an example of one of my ground blinds) after you've identified the buck you are after. Go in on the rainiest or windiest day to set up.

174

At closer range I am trying to identify exact trails the buck is using. I also note what trails other deer in the area are using as I have found mature bucks will usually do their own thing. They are the last to come out and the first to leave, but spooking any deer will let the one you are after know you are there, which, in turn, will probably change his habits.

Once I have a good grasp on where and when the buck is traveling, I go back to Google Earth. I find landmarks and openings in the forest before going in so I have an idea of how far to go in and where bedding areas would most likely be. I have had my best success setting up between bedding and feeding areas.

At this point I switch to trail cam reconnaissance, setting up cameras on trails I have identified. I still keep in mind wind direction and time of day when going in, making sure the wind is not blowing in the direction of bedding areas. I prefer to wear high rubber boots sprayed with sent eliminator spray and a pair of gloves I use only out in the bush and when hunting, also sprayed with scent eliminator spray to lessen the chances of being detected after I leave. I set the trail cameras in spots where I later want to hang a stand or set up a blind. I use whichever weapon I am able to use, depending on season, preferably archery and muzzleloader. I set up about 20-30 yards away from the trail for archery and 20 feet up and approximately 80-90 yards for muzzle loader. This decision is based upon prevailing winds at the location with a tree big enough and facing the right direction for a stand. I also ensure good cover behind the tree even after the leaves have fallen. If a desirable tree cannot be located, I will look for a clump of willows or thick underbrush to conceal a ground blind. After I set up the cameras, I stop scouting feeding areas to lessen my impact there. I generally return every five days to check the cameras to identify the times the buck shows up and what trails he is using. This must be done while being as quiet as possible and still keeping in mind the wind direction and time of day I go in.

When I start to get pictures of the buck I am after, I will then take my stand or blind in to set up—preferably on the rainiest or windiest day I can—again watching wind direction. I find the rain and wind will let me be a little noisier when setting up without spooking deer. I make sure to clip all branches hanging into the trail used to go in and out of stand sites. Move all small sticks and logs off trail to keep noise and scent down in the future while walking in the dark or on calm days.

There are many different strategies and techniques to hunt whitetails, but the most important thing is have fun, respect the outdoors, and share the stories and the experiences with others.

Now that I am ready to hunt, I will refrain from doing so unless the conditions are perfect. The correct wind is the most important factor, and I am always in my stand or blind hours before regular deer movement that I noted on the trail camera pictures. If I am running late, I never go in. I find that if I'm in a hurry, I will be sure to forget something, make noise, leave excessive scent, or a combination of the three. These are all things that can ruin a hunt for the day and possibly push the buck I am after out of area for the season. In one instance my sloppiness caused the buck I was hunting to go completely nocturnal for the remainder of the season. Attention to detail is paramount when hunting mature whitetail bucks. Even if I have not seen a deer during a sit, I never leave until well after dark, and I always move slowly, using a flashlight shining only on the ground directly in front of me. I prefer a flashlight in my hand to a head lamp because head lamps will shine wherever I look, and I don't want my light to shine erratically through brush horizontally. I only need it to see where I am stepping, being sure to be as quiet as possible.

If I believe I have spooked the buck I am after, and he has turned nocturnal or vacated the area (I have done this many times), I will pull out completely as to not educate the buck any more than I already have. As I mentioned earlier, I have hunted some bucks for three—and up to six—years before I had the right opportunity to harvest them, and some are never seen again. It is all part of the hunt.

I draw my most joy from the hunt, the strategy, and the time spent in the woods trying to figure out what a mature trophy buck is thinking. I find these aspects far more rewarding than the harvest itself. That's what keeps me going back into the outdoors chasing whitetails. I always enjoy hearing the stories of hunts—bad or good—from other hunters. The ups and downs of whitetail hunting is the most important thing to try and learn from other hunters in this ever-evolving world of hunting whitetail deer. Even as we get better trail cameras, scent-eliminator sprays, scent-control clothing, faster bows, bigger guns, and numerous other tools to help us, we are still at a disadvantage to a mature whitetail buck. I don't feel these new gadgets are required, but with some time and dedication to the details of deer habits and where they live, anyone can be successful. Keep in mind though that success is not always the harvest of a 200-inch buck. Success is when you feel the rush of adrenaline when a deer walks in front of you and buck fever sets in. Harvest or not, if you are excited telling the story of the hunt, then that is success and that is what will keep you going back for more.

There are many different strategies and techniques to hunt whitetails, but the most important thing is have fun, respect the outdoors, and share the stories and the experiences with others. It is these stories and traditions that help ensure the draw of the deer woods will pull in hunters for generations to come.

Persistence, Patience, and Willpower
Glen Salow | Private Land Success

THE DAY STARTED OFF LIKE MANY OTHERS IN LATE OCTOBER. After a brief conversation with my very understanding wife Ashley, I was off to a new farm for an evening hunt.

I had never hunted this farm before, but I had multiple trail-cam pictures of great deer on this farm and was waiting for the right wind to finally hunt it. It was October 26, and I arrived at the farm with time to spare. I grabbed my gear and began the half-mile walk back to an inside corner of a Conservation Reserve Program (CRP) field. Based off of recent trail cameras pictures, bucks were using this inside corner quite a bit before they went into a cut bean field to feed. I got settled in and it wasn't long before does and young bucks began to filter through.

With about an hour of daylight left I heard a buck grunting behind me. I could not get a good glimpse of him as he was scent-checking some does on the opposite ridge behind me. Once I saw the does head the other way he began heading up the opposite ridge by himself. I gave him two quick grunts and he turned in an instant, heading in my direction. It did not take long for him to close the distance to 30 yards, and before I knew it, I was at full draw as he headed to the left side of the tree. I bleated with my mouth to stop him, settled my 30-yard pin behind his front shoulder and squeezed the release. The arrow found its mark and the 168-inch 4x5 went 50 yards and fell over. This would mark the first of three bucks that grossed in the 160s that I was fortunate to harvest this past season.

I got involved in hunting like most—it was passed down from family. My love for hunting stemmed from my father taking me hunting when I was a kid. I harvested my first Pope and Young buck back in 1995, and from that day on I have always been fascinated with the whitetail deer. For me it's always been the emotional highs and lows that one can experience from hunting the animal that has always captivated me.

Being an avid shed hunter can have high rewards when it comes to being successful in punching your tag.

I have become a very active shed hunter and an official measurer for Boone and Crockett (and many other records-keeping organizations). Being self-employed in the insurance industry and having a wife who understands my passion for hunting allows me to have quite a bit of time in the woods each fall.

Around 2004 I developed a great passion for bowhunting. I have been fortunate since then to harvest some great deer with a bow, including five eligible for the Boone and Crockett records books (one that qualifies for the All-time records book and four that make the Awards book). I have always been a real low-key guy and pretty simple hunter when it comes to my gear and hunting. I have always believed if something is not broken, don't try to fix it. I have come to the conclusion over the years that there are three key components an individual needs to put together every year to consistently harvest Boone and Crockett-caliber deer with a bow. They may all sound fairly simple, but in the grand scheme of things putting all three together is not an easy task.

The 2012 archery season was a great year for me. I was tagged out by November 8 with two great bucks, one of them being my first All-time non-typical Boone and Crockett. It was the latter part of the season when I had a conversation with a close friend who had been hunting dawn to dark for well over a week with no encounters or sightings of any mature bucks. He hunted multiple farms and consistently saw a lot of deer. He rarely got winded and had good entry and exits to most of his stands. From his tone I could tell he was burned out and ready to hang it up for the year. As he told me all this, I simply told him that you cannot harvest what does not exist. He was speechless.

The first key component to harvesting a Boone and Crockett-caliber deer is very, very simple: it has to exist. Now I know many experts all say the same thing: location, location, location. There is no way around that answer, location has the most crucial role in harvesting big deer. Someone once told me that you don't have to be a great hunter to harvest big deer if you have an abundance of them to hunt, and I believe there is some truth to that. I am fortunate that I live in Iowa where the management practices of our state have allowed me the opportunity to have record book deer to pursue. With that said however, I have to admit that every year more and more big deer are harvested in places that were never on the map for book bucks. I believe with the practices of state management and Quality Deer

With proper utilization of your trail cameras, you can usually distinguish a pattern which was the case here with the author's archery harvest on October 26, 2013.

Management Association (QDMA), there are a lot more hot spots out there than people realize, and with proper research you can find those areas.

Now I know many guys who are in the right location, and they simply hunt the same farms year after year. They rarely harvest a book buck, and if they do, it's not consistently. There is no other way around this, you cannot harvest something that does not exist. This is the first key component and the most difficult in my opinion to succeed at, however, there are a few options one can go about in completing this.

The first option is simple, a visual sighting. In my experience, this is the most time-consuming way to ensure the existence of a big deer, but if you have the time and you're persistent, it has proven itself over and over. This is accomplished by simply glassing with good optics, always from a safe distance, and usually from inside a vehicle in the early part of the fall. You want to always remain as far away as possible, especially when glassing from

LEFT: Scouting in the early winter while deer still carry their antlers will give you a higher advantage for success in locating one for the upcoming season.

ABOVE: Finding sheds of Boone and Crockett-caliber deer can sometimes be just as exciting as harvesting the animal.

10/26/2012 4:36 AM

Knowing the existence of a book deer in your hunting area is half the battle when it comes to consistently harvesting book deer.

a vehicle. The last thing you want to do is pull right up to a field and clear all the deer out as you're skidding to a stop.

You want to start scouting like this when all the bucks are still in velvet. Watching bucks in velvet can be a lot of fun too as they always look much bigger than they actually are, so keep that in mind. One can usually find a good bachelor group of bucks in agricultural fields such as soy beans or alfalfa this time of year. But keep in my mind not all deer in velvet feel safe in daylight. And it seems when they shed their velvet, they perform the disappearing act for a week or two, so don't panic, he's not dead, just in hiding. It's also common for deer to disperse to a different core area after they shed their velvet, so you may need some additional time trying to relocate him. If one has the time to scout like this, it can prove very effective if you're persistent and patient.

The second option is shed hunting. You can get a head start on this by doing some scouting from your vehicle. Start glassing agricultural fields in January when most deer are very visible in daylight hours as they are generally run down from the rut and are back into survival mode. When in search of sheds, focus on all southerly slopes, especially those with cedar and locust trees on them and any type of warm grasses. All the waterways and terraces in the agricultural fields are also key areas. I have had quite a few shed seasons in the triple digits, most sheds I spot are 20 to 30 yards out and are in the bedding area or next to the food source. Try to look for four inches of antler and not that 90-incher we all dream about. You will save yourself a lot of walking by carrying a good set of optics with you at all times to glass all the look-alikes. It's also best to shed hunt on gloomy days, especially right after a rain as the sheds will really stick out. Finding a 170-inch-plus set of sheds is a big accomplishment for anyone, but just finding them solves a lot of the puzzle for the upcoming season.

This is also a great time of the year to scout for the next season as all deer sign remains really visible in late winter due to lack of vegetation. You can venture into areas that you would normally never go into during the hunting season. Though it may be unlikely the sheds fall in the deer's core area, you at least have an idea of the section he is living on and you can exercise other options to locate him in the upcoming season.

There have been numerous stories of people finding big sheds and deciding to hunt the area the following year. I recall a hunt from a couple seasons ago with the same scenario, but this time my bow was left in the case and replaced with my muzzleloader. We had just had a major blizzard come through and the interstate was still a mess for travel. I elected to hunt a farm really close to my home that I had always had permission to hunt but rarely did. I carried in a stand and set up in draw that led into a big alfalfa field. This southerly sloped draw had produced many good sheds for me over the years. With a half-hour of light left, a big mature 164-inch 5x5 with a couple burr points came out and gave me a 130-yard shot. Upon recovering the deer, I realized I had picked up a shed off this deer the previous winter not 100 yards from where I harvested him. It's safe to say most hunts won't always turn out this way, but without the evidence of the previous year's sheds, I would have never hunted that farm.

The last option is the trail camera. Trail cameras are probably the number one tool in locating big deer. It's the easiest way to find big deer, and it's a lot of fun. In the average season I will run approximately 15 cameras to cover multiple areas. They save me so much time in trying to locate a big deer to hunt. If you run them correctly, they will do all your scouting for you with little to no pressure on the deer. First, always try position your camera away from the sunrise and sunsets, because there's nothing worse than photos you can't make out due to the sun. I always try to face mine in a northerly direction for best photos and clarity. Placement is usually pretty simple, anytime you have a gate opening between fields or even on a field edge you're going to get pictures of most of the deer in the area. Funnels, water holes or any food plots you may have established are always good spots as well. In many cases you can place an attractant such as a corn pile in front of the camera. I believe if you dump 50 pounds of corn in front of a camera with an average deer population over a two-week period, you will have pictures of all the resident deer in that core area of approximately 60 to 80 acres. (Check with your local games laws first to ensure placing out attractants is legal in your area).

It is important to have good access points to and from your cameras when checking them. The key is you don't want to put any pressure on the deer when setting up or checking your trail cameras. The best way I have found is when I can drive my vehicle right up to them and leave it running while I switch my cards out. If you have to venture into the woods, try to do it during a rain or right before a rain to minimize your scent. I try to place all my cameras out by the end of July, and I won't check them for at least three to four weeks. When you do get the deer you're looking for on camera, there is no need to check it every week. Once the season gets closer, check your cameras more frequently to try to pin down a pattern on a certain deer. You can use your cameras not only to locate deer, but they are a great tool for hunting as well. You can run them throughout the entire season all the way into shed season to get a good idea of what's in store for the following season.

Monitor your cameras as safely as possible throughout the entire season. In some cases bucks will simply just show up for different reasons, it could be for does, a food source, or maybe they have been run out of their core area and they're looking for another one. Time and time again guys harvest book deer that they have never seen before. I recall a hunt from last season where a good friend of mine shot a 172-inch gross 4 by 4 in early November by sitting patiently in a funnel in an area known to produce big deer. He had no history whatsoever of this deer in this area, but his persistence led him to harvest in my opinion, the deer of a lifetime.

Having a name for the deer will always add more to the story line. As shown here in 2011 when the author pursued a deer for two years he had named Picket Fence.

10/27/2012   7:29 AM

Cuddeback

It's important to run your cameras throughout the entire season and make sure your time stamp is always set to the correct time and day as you never know what may show up, which was the case here with this 182-inch mainframe 6x6 the author harvested back in 2012.

A picture will tell you many things. It will usually give you a good idea of the age of the deer, whether he is 3-½ or 4-½ or even 5-½ years old. Certain characteristics of his rack and what he may score, which direction he is heading, whether it be a food source or a bedding area. You can also pick up on certain body markings such as a cut or torn ear. The best thing I like about a trail camera is the time stamp. Is he moving in daylight or is he strictly nocturnal? You can also keep track of the wind direction to see if there is a pattern there. Another thing I will always do is name the deer. Naming deer can be a lot of fun, and I have heard quite a few entertaining names over the years such as Casper or Houdini, just to name a few. This will also help if you have others hunting the same deer and you all share the same name for the deer, but it is mainly for identification purposes in the future whether it be a harvest or picking up his shed antlers. And it will add more to the storyline when the deer is harvested if he has a name.

One of the best things I like about getting pictures of a deer you're after is that it gives you the confidence to stay in the tree stand knowing that the buck you're after is there. A lot of successful hunters have used the trail camera method. A classic case was a deer I scored last year shot by a man named Ben Thomson, who harvested this huge non-typical with unbelievable drop tines during the early muzzleloader season in Iowa. Ben had a CRP field he could hunt and took a chance on it with a couple trail cameras. When he checked his cards from his cameras, he was shocked to see a deer of that caliber. After studying many more pictures he captured of this deer over a couple months, he discovered a pattern. After putting together a strategic plan, he was successful at harvesting the non-typical whitetail on the opening day of the season, which gross scored 246 inches non-typical. Had Ben not used trail cameras, there is a chance he might not have ever known about that deer.

Once you have evidence of a book deer and have secured permission to hunt him, the most difficult task is complete. A lot of people out there want to harvest a book deer, but in reality most people will never get a chance at one, not because they don't exist in their area, but because they don't take the time to find one. With that task completed that leads to the second key component which is, "hunt smart."

When I first started bow hunting many years ago I hunted a 30-acre piece of timber, and I always parked close to the farmer's house. The farmer would sit in his kitchen window sipping his coffee and watch me walk into my stand every time. I always walked in on an old logging road that ran through the east side of his timber. I was completely exposed to everything as I tromped right through it clear to the back to my stand site. Every night the farmer would talk to me about all the deer that ran out of the west side of the timber. Well this became a repetitive thing with him always telling me of my mistakes, and I became irritated with this, to say the least. One day I decided to try something different. I elected to take his advice and walk way out of my way through the bordering agriculture fields and sneak in from the back side. The first time I hunted it that way I had a big 4x4 pushing close to 150 come below my tree at 15 yards. I would like to say that my shot was perfect and the deer went home with me. Unfortunately it did not work out that way, and I got to hear a lot more from the farmer, but this time it was about how I needed more practice with my bow.

The most crucial key to hunting smart is entry and exit to your hunting location. I think this is where most people struggle the most or don't even realize they're educating the deer. Once you educate a specific deer or unknowingly jump him out of his bed, the game is usually over. One of the first things I look at when setting up a stand is entry and exit. If I don't have a great entry and exit, I will usually elect not to hunt that specific area and find a closer alternative. You can usually figure a lot of this out by studying aerial and topographic maps to pinpoint certain areas and preferred entry and exits.

Using the terrain is always the best option for entry and exits such as ditches and creeks. Ditches and ravines always provide great cover when you can walk in them and remain unseen on the way to and from your stand site. Whenever I can use a creek with flowing water, I take advantage of it as walking in water is always quieter than crunchy leaves, and the water will minimize a lot of your scent. Always try to keep the wind in your face when entering and in some cases you may have to walk a ways out of the way to avoid a bedding area or a food source. It's not uncommon for the entry to be different from the exit as well. For example you may walk across an agriculture field to get to your stand for an evening hunt, but when exiting, you may go out of your way to avoid that same agriculture field, because it's always best to avoid going anywhere near a major food source in the cover of darkness. This goes for a morning hunt or after an evening hunt when chances are pretty high you're going to bump and blow out deer. Keep in mind that even putting pressure on the deer that you're not hunting can affect the one deer you're after, so you don't want to blow out does or other bucks that you're not hunting. If you put a lot of pressure on your resident deer, there is not a whole lot there for a buck to stick around for during the rut. Again, avoid any human pressure on all the deer, the lower the pressure, the better the hunting.

Once entry and exit points are established, the next piece of the puzzle is stand sites. I prefer to do this in August as it will give the deer plenty of time to get used to any shooting lanes or other alterations to the land that may have been made. Some may have a different approach to this, but I don't try to be sneaky about it when hanging stands. I usually wear normal street clothes, and I don't worry about making any racket in the woods. In some situations I will even drive my vehicle or ATV right to the tree and leave it run the whole time until I complete my stand set-up. When you use this approach, you are controlled danger and not an uncontrolled danger, meaning the deer know you're there and you're not as much of a threat.

Take for example someone cutting firewood in the woods with a chainsaw. When that person finishes up and leaves, most of the resident deer in that area will come in to investigate as they are a very curious animal. In some cases, being cautious maybe is the best way to go. In that case, I prefer to do stands just like setting up cameras, either during a rain or right before a rain to wash away my scent when I am done.

I always prefer to hang stands at heights from 18 to 20 feet. I always place them 15 to 25 yards off the trail most likely used and preferably in the biggest tree available with the best tree lean for the stand and the best cover for concealment. There is nothing worse than sitting in a tree wishing you had put your stand in the tree 10 feet away because it has a better lean to it and would be more comfortable or it has better cover to it. I also look at a stand site from a few different angles. I want to make sure that the approaching deer cannot see me or make me out but also remain unseen for when they pass by. It's also very important to brush in your stand sites to be more concealed and it takes very little to do this. I will usually use zip ties and any natural cover for this. Oak branches with leaves are best as they will hold their leaves throughout most of the season. And if in pop-up blinds, the same would apply, lots of brushing in and you want to give the deer as much time as possible to get used to them. In most cases at least two to three weeks. And lastly, in certain situations when the season is in full swing, it's important to have a good lightweight set of climbing sticks and lightweight hang-on stand that you can pack in and pack out with you for a quick one-time setup if needed. And always wear a safety harness, the rule I have always had is no harness, no hunt.

> ## TAKE ADVANTAGE OF TERRAIN
> Use a creek with flowing water. Walking in water is always quieter than crunchy leaves, and the water will help minimize your scent.

It's important to always pay attention to your wind and scent. I always tie scentless dental floss on my stabilizer so I always know which way the wind is blowing as my bow is hanging in the tree. It's safe to say most people know how to hunt their areas according to most wind directions—you don't want your wind blowing toward any direction you expect deer to come from or when they pass by. And if your wind switches when in the tree, it's always in your best interest to move to a different tree favored by that wind. A common mistake is not watching your wind when blind calling. I believe that time and again a big mature deer can circle a hunter well out of site and catch your wind. Experience has taught me that when a mature deer winds a hunter at that distance, they normally will not blow at you, and you will not even know you were just busted. It's important to always make sure that with any blind calling you do, there is no possible way for the deer to get downwind of you without going through one of your shooting lanes first.

As far as the timing of the hunt, it is pretty simple. During the rut, the more time you can put in the tree, the higher the odds of success. For me the best time to harvest book deer has always been the last week of October or the first cold front of October. There is always something about the first front of October that seems to get all the mature deer on their feet in daylight. If you run your cameras throughout the season, pictures on your camera will reveal this to you as well. For the best results, I always try to hunt a staging area right next to a food source during the first front of October. With that said, all but one of the five Boone and Crockett deer I have harvested have been in the last week of October. I believe the bucks are getting anxious for the approaching rut at this time and are on their feet just a few days prior to getting with that first doe. It's not normally all-day sits, but for me it has been a proven method, especially on the evening hunts. This past season I harvested my first buck on October 26 and the second buck on October 29. The buck I harvested on the 29th I actually passed up on the 25th. But when I watched the video footage that night I told myself if he comes back, I won't pass him again. Fortunately for me, I did not have to wait long for a second chance.

But don't let November fool you as it's probably the number one time that most hunters harvest big deer, and I would assure you there are more successful hunters in November than October. Many people have told me if they had just a couple days to hunt out of the year, it would be November 6-8. During the rut, I mainly hunt funnels and bedding areas on all-day sits, with my most successful times of action being between 9:00 a.m. and 2:00 p.m. This is the only time of year I prefer to do any calling, and it's usually only when I visually see a deer I am after and know with certainty that he is going the opposite direction before I attempt anything. If he is with a doe, usually any calling will only educate him and push him farther way. When I hit the later part of the rut as it is winding down, I will focus back on the food sources, mainly on evening hunts. Even though most all of my success has been in October, I will say that the most exciting days of action I have ever had in the field were always in November during the rut.

Now that you have evidence of the deer you're after, your stands are set, and you have planned out all your entry and exit points, what's left? The last key component sounds very simple: you have to "harvest that deer." Sounds easy, right? Well, there are two pieces of this puzzle. Let's start with the first one. How many times have you heard, "I hit a limb or I just grazed him," or as I told that farmer, "He jumped the string." The key here is you have to put a fatal shot on the deer when it presents itself, and that's not as easy it as sounds. I'll be the first to admit, I have had my fair share of misses and poor shots over the years. I guess that's why they call it hunting and not harvesting. But there are things that can be done to make that shot more favorable for you when it needs to count.

The main thing I do that has helped me tremendously is I always harvest antlerless deer in the early part of the season. I have always hunted special management or urban hunt areas whose goal is antlerless deer harvest. I have learned over the years that shooting antlerless deer in the early part of the season has made it a walk in the park when a big mature buck presents you with a shot. Now every situation is different, but remaining calm is easier said than done. I always try to focus on the shot and not pay too much attention to the antlers. If you just stare at the antlers, it always seems something will go horribly wrong. Most importantly when that buck does approach you, there is no need to second-guess yourself if he is a shooter or not, as you already know the deer from your scouting methods. You will have more time to prepare for your shot and make it count.

Knowing where you hit the animal is very crucial as well. You can improve the visibility of your arrow flight by cresting your arrows with bright colors and using vanes of bright colors. Over the years I have always preferred white arrow crests and white vanes with orange or pink nocks. Lighted nocks are probably the best tool for knowing exactly where you hit the animal, and keep in mind Pope and Young will now accept animals harvested with lighted nocks as well.

Let's face it though, not every shot will be a quick recovery within minutes or you watch the animal expire from the comfort of your tree stand. Usually if something can go wrong, it will, hit a limb or misjudge the yardage are all very common things that will happen at some point. If you don't see the deer fall over or hear it crash or you know with certainty

It's sometimes the simple things that will give you the higher advantage when your shot matters the most.

the shot was perfect, it's always wise to give it at least a few hours. Try to find your arrow first—the most important thing if you don't know where your shot placement was. Going in for the recovery too soon is a mistake we have all made, and more times than not it will result in a lost animal. Patience is key in questionable shots, and usually the results will be more in your favor for a recovery. For anything that is not in the heart and lung area, I prefer to wait 18 to 24 hours, and in some cases that may still require a follow-up shot. If the trail does get lost, don't expand your grid search more than 300 yards from the initial shot right away, in most cases if the deer has expired, he is usually within 300 yards of that initial shot. One of the things I have done that's helped me when a shot presents itself is a sticker I have placed on my bow riser that says "pick a spot." And believe it or not, at full draw I see it every time before I squeeze my release.

Obviously, shooting a lot in the off-season will help accuracy as well. When you have confidence in your equipment and your aim, that makes it all the better when your moment of truth arrives. I try to shoot a couple nights a week, 40 to 50 shots at 40 yards every time. I rarely shoot deer as far as 40 yards, but if I practice all the time at 40 yards and get that down to a baseball-sized group, then shooting at 20 and 30 yards is a chip shot. It's also very important to continue to shoot during the season as well.

The second piece of this puzzle that will take a lot of willpower is passing up other deer. If you have a Boone and Crockett deer to hunt, and harvesting it is your goal, then it's pretty simple you have to pass the 150 to 160 class deer. Trust me, this is no easy thing to do. I have had years where I regretted it and some years with high rewards. Being committed to one single animal will have its challenges. I remember a buck I hunted a few years ago that I had named Footer due to the inside spread of his rack being over two feet wide. It was the first cold front of October, and it was one I will always remember. A friend wanted to tag along to film, and I am glad I accepted because the footage from that night turned out incredible. The evening hunt started out great, as bucks were all on their feet. With the last hour of light left I had a big mature 4x4 come by at 15 yards and make a scrape. He stood in the shooting lane for a couple minutes working a scrape. I estimated him close to the 160-mark, and as hard as it was, I passed up the deer because he was not the buck I was after. Not long after, another buck came through that I had some history with. He was a big 6x5 that would gross score in the mid-160s. Once again, I made the tough decision to pass him up. It was not easy to do this, but I knew Footer was close to that 200-inch mark and that's what I wanted. My buddy thought I had lost my mind, literally.

A little over a week later, from that same tree on October 26, I harvested Footer at 15 yards. He ended up grossing 194 inches, with a couple broken points. He netted 168-6/8 as a typical 5x5 and had an inside spread over 24 inches. My view on this was simple. I believed that I would have more opportunities in my life to harvest 160-class deer but not very many opportunities to possibly harvest a 200-inch deer, so I chose that year to harvest him or nothing. Fortunately it worked out for me. Had I not harvested him that season, that 4x4 would have been a hard one to forget anytime soon.

So in conclusion if you can succeed at all three key elements your results will speak for themselves. A prime example I have of this is from the 2012 archery season when everything came together. I had two buck tags for the archery season, one being valid in an urban hunt area and the other being valid statewide. It was the middle of July when I had gathered all my cameras for testing and replaced them all with new batteries. Once all my cameras were placed out, I did not pull my first card until mid-August. On the first card I had one really good deer in one area I hunt, and he became known as Big Moe. I estimated his score based on the trail cam pictures to gross B&C, but I was not confident on him netting it. In my other areas, I had four other bucks on my camera that would gross-score between 170 and 200, with one for sure making the book. I named him Bruiser, and another one very close to his size on a different farm that I named Kodak since he loved the camera so much. To say the least I was ready for October to get here.

Once we hit the middle of October, I put a lot of focus on Big Moe. I had pinned down his core area, and he was becoming a very predictable deer. My access to check the cameras was perfect, due to the drought we had that year, I could get in and out totally undetected by using a very deep, dry creek bed. I also realized that over the past two years I had gotten pictures of Big Moe but only in velvet and under the cover of darkness—then he would disappear for the rest of the season. But this year was different. It was obvious he was here to stay.

My entry and exit was so good I started checking a couple of my cameras every few days starting around October 20, hoping to get a picture of him in daylight. With the pattern I had on him, it was very tempting to hunt him, but I had no daylight pictures at all, he was totally nocturnal to this point.

Finally on October 30, I snuck in and checked a camera with my gear in tow. I scrolled through the card to find out I had a picture of him that morning at 9:00 a.m., the first time ever in daylight. The direction he was headed based on the picture gave me a good idea of where he was bedded. I had a stand site about 150 yards from where I thought he was, and the wind was just right. The stand was located right next to a big creek with steep banks on the back side of the tree that made for a perfect funnel. It took me some time to sneak into my tree but I finally got settled in without alerting any deer. The plan was to sit quietly and based on his pattern my cameras had come up with, he should come by me before the day's end, just hopefully in daylight. I had quite a few deer come

FIELD PHOTOGRAPHY TIPS

- Clean up the blood, tuck in the tongue and flatten out any roughed hair on the deer.
- Take your photo in a natural environment where a deer would live.
- If you're wearing a hat, tip the bill of your hat up to avoid shadows, and try to face the sun.
- Put the deer in a bedded position with both of his front legs bent over and touching his belly.
- For the best pictures, try to get the head and antlers of the deer skylined with the upper third of your body skylined as well.
- Consider including your rifle, bow, etc. somewhere in the picture.
- Shoot your photos from a very low point off the ground and at a slightly upward angle to get the skylined picture of yourself and your deer.
- The goal here is to avoid the pictures with your buddy's beer cans all over the truck bed as you pose with your harvest.

If you have the willpower to pass other bucks, your success will speak for itself when you close the deal on the one you're after.

through early, and things were looking good. With about 30 minutes of light left, I heard the famous crunch of the leaves behind me, and low and behold, Big Moe was heading my way. I quickly glassed him to confirm it was him, and then got my bow in hand. He was trying to approach my downwind side and was doing a pretty good job at it as there was a very small 30-yard gap between my tree and the creek bank. As he approached my wind, I came to full draw. I could smell the Ozone coming out of my Ozonics as I bleated to stop him. I held my 20-yard pin behind his shoulder and squeezed the release. After the shot, he took off with his tail up, which made me extremely nervous. He then stopped after about 40 yards, began to side-step and just fell over. What a relief and what a sight that was. I made a few calls from the tree to share the news with my wife and friends. After that, I wasted little time getting down to take a look at him. Once I got up to him I was totally shocked at how big he actually was; I had drastically underestimated his size. He was a huge deer carrying a typical 6x5 frame at 185-inch's with multiple burr points, he gross-scored 205-5/8 and netted 196 non-typical. My first All-time B&C buck, to say I was excited would be an understatement.

I took the day of October 31 to get some good harvest photos and get him caped out—which leads me to a quick suggestion. Being an official scorer, one of the biggest regrets I hear from hunters is not getting good harvest pictures. If you harvest a Boone and Crockett deer—or anything considered a trophy for that matter—try to do your best to get some good harvest photos. One of the best photos I prefer is a sky lined photo, and it's pretty simple actually. First thing for any photo is to clean up the blood, tuck in the tongue and flatten out any roughed hair on the deer. Always try to take your harvest photos in a natural environment where a deer would live. If you're wearing a hat, tip the bill of your hat up to avoid shadows, and try to face the sun. Put the deer in a bedded position with both of his front legs bent over and touching his belly while you get in a seated position behind the deer. For the best pictures, try to get the head and antlers of the deer sky lined with the upper third of your body sky lined as well. Try to also include your weapon of harvest somewhere in the picture. You will want to shoot your photos from a very low point off the ground and at a slightly upward angle to get the sky lined picture of yourself and your deer. There are many good ways to take a good photo, and this is one I have always preferred and have taken a liking to. The goal here is to avoid the pictures with your buddy's beer cans all over the truck bed as you pose with your harvest.

I wasted little time focusing on my other tag as I had a similar scenario going on at a couple different farms with two deer I named Bruiser and Kodak. I was informed just a few days before I harvested Big Moe that Kodak was harvested by the neighbor already, and he ended up just shy of the 200-inch mark as a non-typical. To make matters worse, I had multiple pictures of him in daylight starting around mid-October. But I still had Bruiser to pursue, so my confidence remained high. I figured he would net in the upper 190s non-typical, but the amazing thing was his body size—he had to be one of the biggest-bodied deer I ever got pictures of. I hunted all day on November 1, and the whole day was really slow. I elected that night after the hunt to drive my truck into the field to check a couple cameras that were on the edge of the field to get a better feel of what was going on. Later that night when I went through the cards I realized the last pictures I had of Bruiser was around October 20. The interesting thing was a new deer had showed up now, and I was getting pictures of him every other day starting right around the 20th as well. He was a mature mainframe 6x6 with a couple abnormal points, and I figured he would gross in the 180's. I figured a couple things may have happened to Bruiser. One, he got harvested already, or two, he was not aggressive at all and was run off by this new buck.

When using the terrain to your advantage when entering and exiting your stands the results can be very rewarding as shown here with the author's 205-inch, non-typical from 2012.

I was able to get in a couple hunts over the next few days but proved unsuccessful in punching my tag. Finally on November 8, I caught the break I needed. At first light a doe came through with a big 150-class 4x4 in tow. He was very tempting to shoot actually. But it seemed every half hour another buck would come through, and he would chase them off. I passed up the 4x4 a few different times, and I filmed him breeding the doe in front of my tree once. There were at least a half-dozen other bucks that bedded down within view of my tree trying to slip in on the doe from time to time. This went on all morning long and the action was really intense. Then at 11:30, I looked up in the opposite end of the field to see a big-framed deer headed my way. I got the camera on him and realized it was the 6x6 I had gotten pictures of recently. He saw a couple of the small bucks standing by my tree, and he wasted little time closing the distance to run them off. The problem was I got caught up using the camera and filmed him coming the whole way into 25 yards. Just as he was about to slip away, I finally got my bow up and drawn on him right before he passed by me. I bleated at him to stop him and squeezed the release. The arrow flew true and I watched as he crashed off 100 yards to his final resting place near the field edge. Once again I wasted little time in getting down for the recovery.

He turned out to be a great deer, sporting a 170-inch 6x6 typical frame with 12 inches in abnormal points, giving him a gross score of 182-4/8 and a net of 177 non-typical. I know he did not make the Boone and Crockett records book, but it was close enough for me. I was also later advised that the deer I named Bruiser had relocated about a mile-and-a-half away from the farm I hunted at the end of October for reasons unknown to me. My only suspicion was the buck I killed was more aggressive and ran him off.

The 2012 archery season was a great year for me and I have been blessed with others with similar results over the years. I have done this by being persistent and patient and having the willpower to accept defeat at the end of the season should I pursue one specific animal without success. The three key components mentioned here all sound very, very simple. But trust me, putting the three together every year is not an easy task. However if you can, I am very confident the chances are pretty high you will harvest a Boone and Crockett-caliber deer. And one last thing I never mentioned, let's not forget a little luck on your side never hurts. Lord knows I have had my fair share of it over the years, but that's a story for another day.

Statistics Behind the Trophies
Justin Spring | B&C Assistant Director of Big Game Records

BOONE AND CROCKETT RECORDS ARE MAINTAINED TO GAUGE successes and failures of wildlife management. This was the original intent of the system and the reason today that we spend the time and effort to ensure the quality of data points used, so what better place than a guide to whitetail hunting to take you through the numbers and trends we see in North America?

To start, let's consider the basics of the scoring system and why we record what we do. One of the biggest criticisms of Boone and Crockett's scoring is about deductions. We hear "Why not give the buck credit for what he grew?" and "Deductions are inappropriate on a rack; since it's there, score it." Our methodology is steeped in biology. In the natural world, bilateral symmetry is the predominant normal form. From humans to fish, bugs to deer, all animals show perfect symmetry in their ideal state. In the event a particular animal shows an abnormality on a side, it is considered different or non-typical. The same is said with the development of deer antlers. In a perfect situation, the deer will grow massive, symmetrical antlers. Any abnormalities to this typical pattern are generally caused by some form of stressor either during development or potentially some type of damage to the pedicle, in which case the abnormalities return year after year. Particular gene combinations can take effect where every few generations a unique configuration shows up in a population. But biology shows us that if this mutation was advantageous, it would continue on and allow a higher breeding ability of the animal. Population-wide mutations are very rare and in most cases can be traced to a genetic bottleneck where a particular buck with a recessive antler configuration did the majority of

Have you recently harvested a buck that makes B&C's Big Game records book? Odds are it was a nice, sunny day and you were shooting a .30-06 like this hunter. Chad L. Widness harvested his typical whitetail scoring 190-1/8 points in Minnesota during the 2010 season.

breeding so the dominant genes show a non-typical phenotype far more commonly. Research done both in the United States and in Europe shows that stressors trigger antler abnormalities. Such stressors could include infection, injury sustained from excessive fighting for breeding rights—especially common in overpopulated areas—or simply an injury caused by human interaction such as a car collision or getting hung up in a fence. The basis of B&C's scoring system is to rank trophies higher that exhibit the favorable, "perfect" traits for the species.

Now that you know what B&C is looking for and have a basic understanding that the quantity of entries should correlate to better management, let's look at some trends. First, not all locations that have whitetail deer have been included in all the graphs. We chose to use a diverse cross-section of U.S. deer-hunting states. This is in no way discounts them as some of the best hunting locations to take a mature trophy whitetail, rather an omission for space constraints. While critiquing numbers and trends among entries, we will delve into more obscure data that the club attaches to entries and see if any trends may appear that could help you on your next hunt.

First let's look at the gradient of entries in five-year increments from 1950 through 2013 (Chart A). Keep in mind the last data point is an incomplete number (we are in that current period as this book goes to print), and we will not get the complete picture until approximately a year after the last included date as entry times vary from 61 days until a couple years after harvest to obtain an accepted entry.

While examining the data, the first thing one will notice is that a major spike occurs from 1985-1989. This is intriguing, and it's worth noting that the idea of allowing deer to grow began to take hold in the late 1980s. It could also be attributed to the fact that the Club began separating Awards and All-time minimum scores in the 1980s. In order to weed this factor out, I calculated entries using only the highest All-time minimum entry score—170 for typical and 195 for non-typical (Chart B).

What this shows us is that from 1985-1989 the number of entries began to skyrocket. The interesting aspect is that this coincides with a major mule deer population decline. Of the cross-section of the states selected, only a couple also have mule deer, and no definitive pattern appears in those. Therefore, I do not feel we could argue the whitetail population greatly expanded to fill a void left by mule deer as the explosion is all across the U.S. (though it is an interesting observation to contemplate).

My first thought to try to explain the 1980s spike was a major reduction in hunting participation; i.e., fewer hunters in the field would allow bucks to achieve an older age class. To test this hypothesis, I explored the United States Fish and Wildlife Service (USFWS) data, and while hunter numbers did fluctuate, the data showed a decrease from nearly 16.7 million licensed hunters in 1981 to 14.7 million in 2003—a 12 percent reduction. That corresponded to an increase in trophy entries of nearly four times (400 percent) during that same time period. While there appears to be a correlation I don't feel a 12 percent reduction in hunters would result in a 400 percent increase. Something changed on a national scale, and the resulting increase in trophies is astonishing. My gut tells me that hunter selection is a major driving force.

When analyzing harvest locations, the states with the greatest increase in trophies are Iowa and Illinois. The farming practices and habitat in these states allow hunters access to the majority of the deer population. Therefore, I attribute the explosion of entries in the mid to late 1980s to a change in hunter selection where deer were allowed to reach an age beyond just legal to be considered for harvest. My argument here is strengthened by states such as Maine and Minnesota. Traditionally these big-woods states have plugged away with a relatively static number of entries. Historically these areas were the big buck hot spots with many deer living their entire existence without being seen by hunters, thanks to good habitat cover. These were the only locations where a deer could reach maturity before being shot—and still produce trophy whitetails, though not near the rate of the newcomer states where I hypothesize the change in hunter selection. A good case study includes trends in deer entries from Pennsylvania. Historically, Pennsylvania's hunting regulations had no antler restrictions, and it was not known as a trophy-producing area. A fairly recent change in policy has added an antler-point restriction, and as such I expect to see an increase in Keystone State trophies as its deer population is allowed to mature.

This transitions us into our more recent comparison of trophy information. Boone and Crockett has been collecting additional information on trophies since the 16th Big Game Awards Period (1974-1976), but this is the first time many of these statistics have been released to the public. It should be noted that although information has been collected for 40 years, additional questions have been added to the information sheet

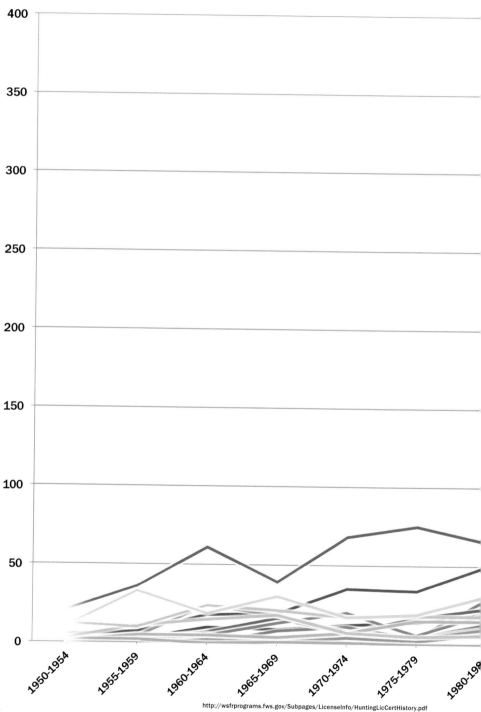

CHART A: Whitetail Deer Entries based on Awards Book Minimums.

Combined totals for typical and non-typical whitetail deer entries for 16 states (160 points for typical, and 185 for non-typical). NOTE: The final date range is incomplete due to timing of deer seasons and B&C required drying period of 60 days.

http://wsfrprograms.fws.gov/Subpages/LicenseInfo/HuntingLicCertHistory.pdf

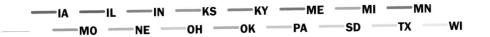

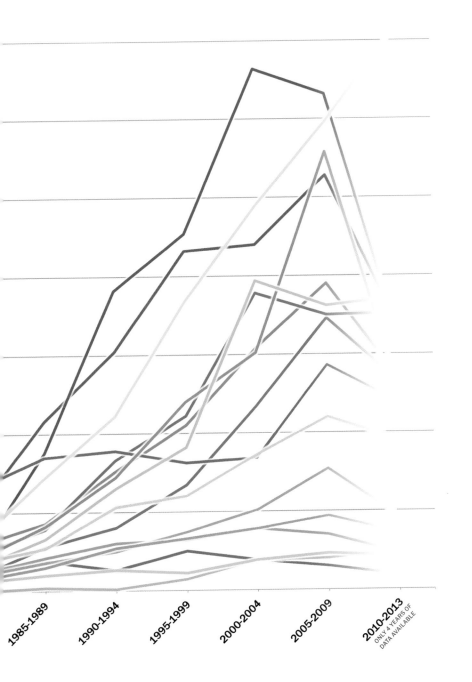

CHART B: Whitetail Deer Entries based on All-time Minimums.

Combined totals for typical and non-typical whitetail deer entries for 16 states (170 points for typical and 195 points for non-typical). Data through 2009 only, since the last five-year increment is not complete.

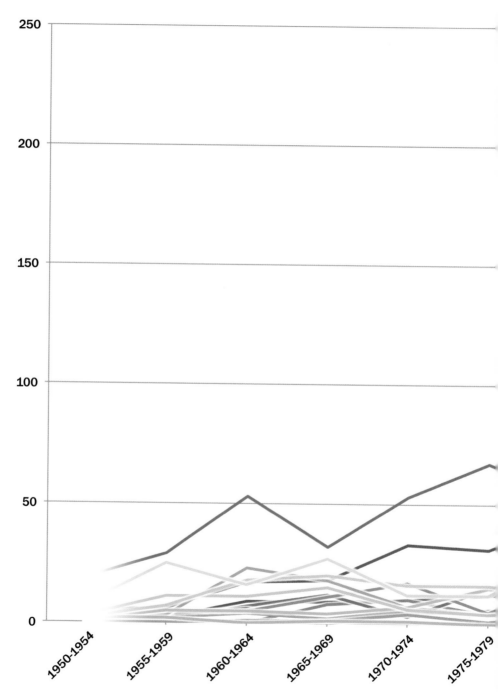

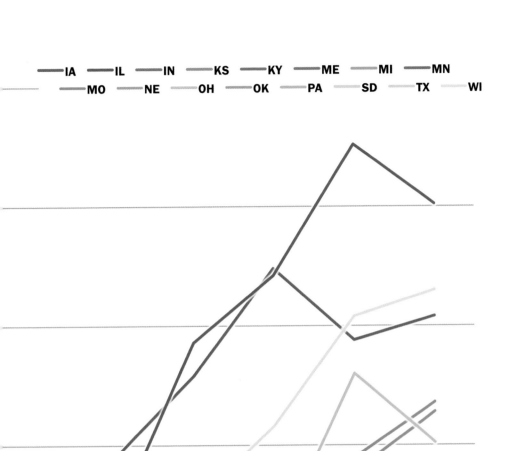

CHART C: Private vs. Public Land Whitetails

Percentage of B&C whitetail entries taken on private versus public lands. Data from 2010 through 2013.

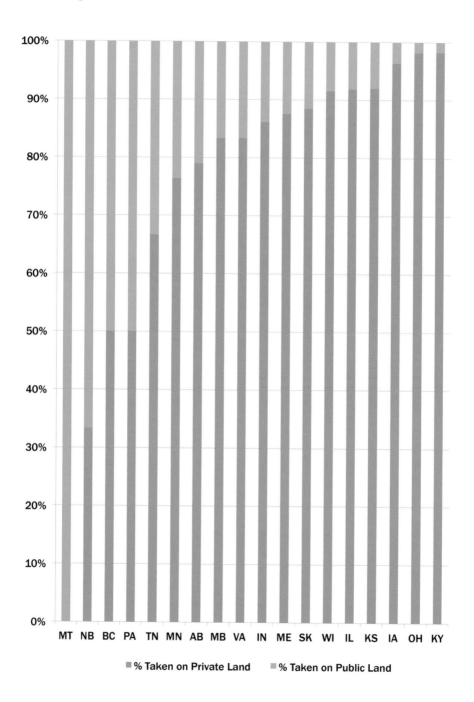

■ % Taken on Private Land   ■ % Taken on Public Land

over time, therefore not all the data sets are complete from the early years. All graphs include the sample size that was used to derive the data.

PUBLIC AND PRIVATE OWNERSHIP DIFFERENCES

It is worth noting that while the vast majority of whitetails are taken on private land, a public land trophy is not impossible. Chart C is slightly misleading as it shows 100 percent of Montana trophies on public land. This is because Montana does not produce many entries, and the only one with ownership information happened to be a deer harvested on public land. The public lands of Wisconsin and Minnesota are still producing the occasional entry for the hunter that puts in his time and effort. Percentage-wise they may not be the leaders, but in numbers of trophies entered from public lands, they top the list. One that is surprising is Idaho. While I know some deer entries have come from public lands, our records do not show any public-land trophies in the book. One factor here may be that many Idaho deer are found on timber company lands—and while technically private, they are open to public hunting. I dislike hypothesizing on trends, but I would love to be able to glean this information from historic entries and see if there has been a major shift to private land. This would help explain whether hunters have been selectively harvesting to maintain management quotas in recent years, or if whitetail deer have just become resilient to human disturbances and adapted to a changing human footprint on their habitat. This is why I mentioned earlier that when mule deer declines started, whitetail populations seemed to start rising. Could it be that whitetails deal with human interference better than other ungulates, resulting in vast amounts of land habitable only to whitetail deer?

> **PRIVATE VS. PUBLIC LAND**
>
> Six hundred and seventy-eight whitetail entries include information on public or private land. Five percent of our entries have ownership included, and they are all 28th and 29th Awards Period entries.

WEATHER CONDITIONS

The next several pages include graphs derived from our weather condition data at time of harvest. We ask hunters for information on the temperature, wind speed, precipitation, and cloud cover when their trophies are harvested. These data are far more complete with the more recent entries.

WEATHER CONDITIONS: CLOUD COVER

Our Hunter, Guide, and Hunt Information form asks each trophy owner about the weather conditions when they harvested their buck. We provide three options for sky conditions: sunny/clear, light overcast, or heavy overcast. Roughly 38 percent of whitetail entries have this data available to analyze.

SKY CONDITION	# TROPHY ENTRIES
Sunny/Clear	2,881
Light Overcast	2,165
Heavy Overcast	611

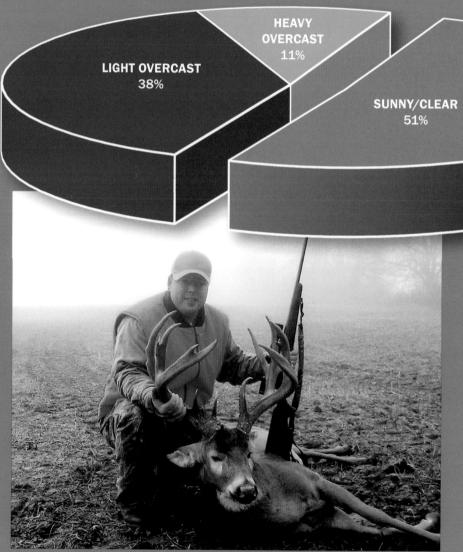

HEAVY OVERCAST – Brandon W. Banks | non-typical | Missouri | 2009 | 196-6/8 points

SUNNY/CLEAR – Raymond N. Andersen | typical | Wisconsin | 2012 | 160-2/8 points

WEATHER CONDITIONS: PRECIPITATION

Our hunter, guide, and hunt information form asks each trophy owner about the weather conditions at the time of harvest. We provide four options for precipitation: none, lightly raining, heavily raining, lightly snowing, heavily snowing.

B&C records include nearly 8,000 whitetail trophies with precipitation data. Approximately 600 whitetail trophy records list some precipitation, so even though the numbers are slightly tough to interpret, the data show it is far less likely for a hunter to kill a book-qualifying whitetail deer in the rain or snow. This really comes as no surprise as many hunters firmly believe deer hunker down in poor weather waiting to move about and feed before or after a weather system moves through.

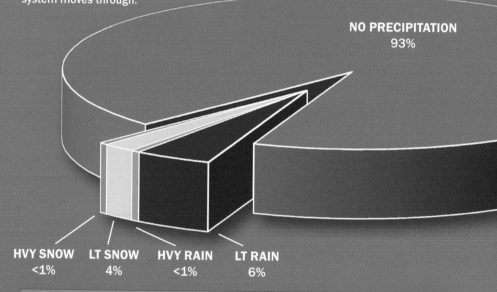

NO PRECIPITATION
93%

HVY SNOW   **LT SNOW**   **HVY RAIN**   **LT RAIN**
<1%   **4%**   **<1%**   **6%**

NO PRECIPITATION – David A. Comer | non-typical | Illinois | 2013 | 194-5/8 points

HEAVY SNOW – David Novak | non-typical | British Columbia | 2010 | 196-7/8 points

Statistics show that it won't likely be raining or snowing when you shoot your trophy buck... at least 93 percent of the time!

However, if there is some type of precipitation, it breaks down like this...

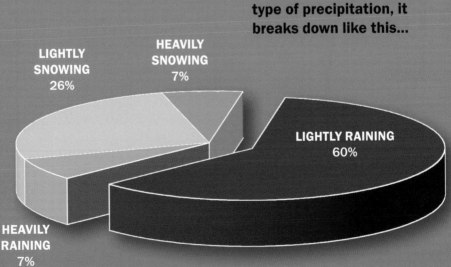

LIGHTLY SNOWING
26%

HEAVILY SNOWING
7%

LIGHTLY RAINING
60%

HEAVILY RAINING
7%

WEATHER CONDITIONS: WIND

The wind speed graph is also interesting. The number of entries with wind speeds of 0-5 mph are probably high because of how data was historically reported, but a look at the data clearly indicates the higher the wind speed, the fewer the trophies taken. To sum this one up: don't hunt in heavy wind.

WIND SPEED (MPH)	# OF TROPHIES TAKEN
0-5	6,914
6-10	601
11-15	261
16-20	172
21-25	78
26-30	56
31-35	13
36-40	10
41+	3

As expected, the wind is a major factor!

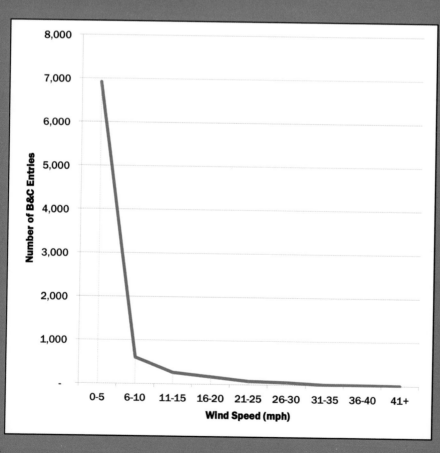

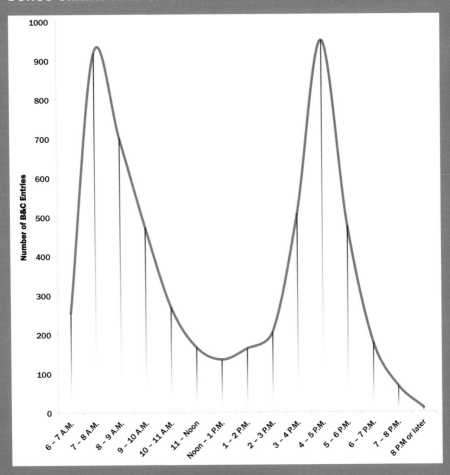

The graph above illustrates, in hourly increments, the time of day a deer was harvested for nearly 5,500 whitetail trophy entries. Includes all methods of take and excludes picked-up trophies.

EVENING – Alberto Bailleres
typical | Texas | 2012
178-6/8 points.

WEATHER CONDITIONS: TEMPERATURE

The final graph from supplementary information is the air temperature when a deer was harvested. These data points were all entered into our system in recent years and are more precise than past entries. Therefore, in my opinion, this is a very accurate demographic of average temperatures across the board for all entries. The trend line displayed on the graph is more for reference; statistically it may not be relevant, though it is interesting when looking at all the entries in the records book.

TEMPERATURE (F)	# OF TROPHIES TAKEN
Colder than -10°	21
-10° – 0°	20
1° – 10°	24
11° – 20°	82
21° – 30°	197
31° – 40°	215
41° – 50°	247
51° – 60°	109
61° – 70°	52
71° – 80°	19
81° and warmer	3

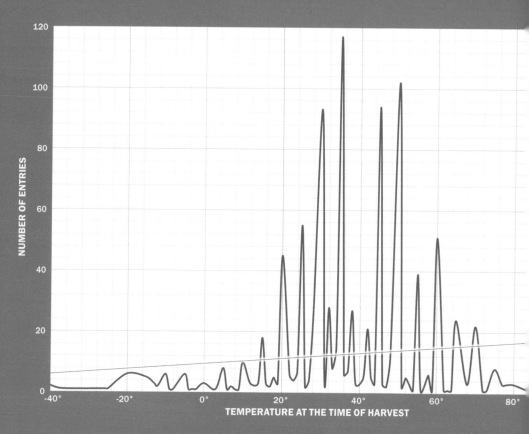

NUMBER OF ENTRIES

TEMPERATURE AT THE TIME OF HARVEST

WARM – Kenneth D. Fulton | non-typical | Kansas | 2012 | 195-5/8 points

COLD – Mike T. Zimmerman | non-typical | Iowa | 2009
196-2/8 points

METHOD OF TAKE

Whenever the topic of hunting whitetails comes up, there is always going to be the discussion of the perfect caliber to take a whitetail buck. When considering only whitetail deer entered in Boone and Crockett records with method-of-take information attached, the .30-06 Springfield is the caliber at the top of the list. In fact, the .30-06 alone actually accounts for more entries than each of the following methods: muzzleloader, handgun, or crossbow. However, at 596 entries, the .30-06 falls behind all combined archery entries (1,317) and shotgun-taken trophies (1,021). I would surmise that the shotgun numbers are that high purely because of the fact that certain states don't allow centerfire rifles for deer hunting. An in-depth breakdown of gauge sizes reveals nearly all shotgun hunters are shooting a 12 gauge. We are currently collecting demographics on archery trophies, including compound versus traditional and draw weights, but I have not been able to locate any insightful trends that may help the hunter, other than the majority of deer are taken with compounds. In states that allow crossbows during archery season, the crossbows are favored and account for more entries, but these states still have plenty of hand-drawn bow entries as well.

That being said, why is the .06 the hands-down winner when it comes to taking trophy whitetail deer across North America? In order to begin this discussion, we must first set some ground rules. Depending on who you ask or what you read, the minimum foot pounds of energy required to kill a deer usually falls into the 900-1,000 foot pounds range. Only once did I feel that my bullet did not have enough energy to do the job with a single well-placed shot in the vitals and back. In that instance, calculating my theoretical energy value, the bullet struck the buck right at or slightly below 900 fps. I did end up putting my tag on this buck, and though I feel the first shot would have been lethal given some additional time, a follow-up shot was necessary at a closer range to quickly and humanely kill the buck. Remember though that this is the energy required for a bullet to inflict the necessary trauma to quickly kill an animal. An archery-taken trophy is not killed by mass trauma, so when you realize the kinetic energy of your broadhead is far below the numbers mentioned above, that is like comparing

SHOT DISTANCE

Across all B&C categories, 75 percent of trophies are taken at a distance of 100 yards or less.

CALIBER PERFORMANCE AT 100 YARDS

CALIBER	BULLET WT.	MUZZLE VELOCITY (fps)	BALLISTIC COEFFICIENT	FPS @ 100 YARDS	YARDAGE FALLS BELOW 1,000 FPS
.223 Rem.	60 Gr.	3,000	.228	886	100
.243	80 Gr.	3,200	.310	1,465	300
	100 Gr.	3,000	.384	1,674	400
.250 Savage	100 Gr.	2,700	.377	1,344	300
.257 Roberts	100 Gr.	3,000	.377	1,668	400
.25-06	100 Gr.	3,200	.377	1,905	450
	115 Gr.	3,000	.389	1,930	500
.260 Rem.	100 Gr.	3,200	.326	1,852	400
	125 Gr.	2,900	.449	1,603	450
.264 Rem. Mag	100 Gr.	3,400	.326	2,097	450
	130 Gr.	3,100	.449	1,740	500
.270 Win.	130 Gr.	3,000	.416	2,207	600
	150 Gr.	2,800	.465	2,250	650
7mm-08	120 Gr.	3,050	.417	2,109	550
	150 Gr.	2,700	.456	2,083	550
7mm Rem. Mag	140 Gr.	3,100	.485	2,602	750
	160 Gr.	2,900	.531	2,629	800
.30-.30 Win.	170 Gr.	2,000	.252 (round nose)	1,099	150
	160 Gr.	2,000	.330 (FTX tipped)	1,117	150
.308 Win.	150 Gr.	2,800	.435	2,227	600
	180 Gr.	2,500	.507	2,168	650
.30-06	150 Gr.	2,900	.435	2,394	650
	180 Gr.	2,700	.507	2,538	750
.300 Win. Mag. or .300 WSM	150 Gr.	3,200	.435	2,928	750
	180 Gr.	3,000	.507	3,149	900
.338 Win. Mag	180 Gr.	3,100	.372	3,206	700
	225 Gr.	2,800	.550	3,456	>1000

apples to oranges . Keep in mind, I am presenting general numbers in terms of bullet availability and keeping pressures and recommended loads well below the maximums suggested in my reference reloading manuals. For the sake of this chapter, we will use 1,000 foot pounds as our minimum lethal amount of energy required just to be safe. So where do the common calibers fall at 100 yards?

In terms of lethal power, all the calibers in the chart on page 221 are more than adequate to humanely kill deer at the common distances encountered in most whitetail hunting situations. Interestingly if you look at the breakdown of bullet diameters in terms of the number of whitetail entered in B&C, the .308, or 30-caliber bullet, hands-down owns this breakdown. This bullet is obviously effective but far larger than necessary to bring down even the largest North American whitetails. It is worth noting that modern reloading practices and cartridge design have given the hunter numerous options and many of the old-guard calibers have fallen slightly to the wayside. I am always surprised that one in particular, the .250 Savage, has fallen so far out of use. When this caliber came out, it was touted as the first production rifle to exceed a muzzle velocity of 3,000 fps with an 87-grain bullet. A look at the chart on page 228 shows the breakdown of bullet diameters listed on trophy entries.

The .277 category is dominated by the .270 Winchester; .284 is made up of the 7mm Mags and a few 7mm-08s; the .308 caliber has the .30-06; .300 Win. Mag., .300 WSM, .30-30 Winchester, and .300 Weatherby, which all fall in the top individual caliber choices. In fact, in B&C's overall data set, if one lumps the number of trophies taken with one of the .300 Magnums together, they bypass the .30-06 entries.

When looking at the numbers, nothing stands out as all that surprising other than the .300 WSM, which can give the .30-06 a run for the title as the best all-around gun. The ballistics of the .300 WSM nearly mimic those of the .300 Win. Mag. but create those velocities and energies with less power, making the cartridge more efficient with less recoil. You may say that is all well and good, but the .300 Win. Mag. punishes your shoulder. However, let's compare published reloading data in *Nosler's Reloading Manual No. 6* of the .300 Win. Mag., .300 WSM, and the .30-06 Springfield.

Looking at these numbers, it comes as no surprise that the .300 WSM has surged toward the top of the lists in numerous categories. It is the same bullet as the .30-06—which has been proven to take all game animals in North America—though its case allows a shorter bolt throw and the increase in charge of only 7 grains gains the user nearly 260 fps at the muzzle for this particular powder.

CALIBER	RECOMMENDED CHARGES IN THE NOSLER MANUAL	LISTED VELOCITIES
.30-06	57.5 – 61.5 grains	2,776 – 2,982
.300 Win. Mag.	72.5 – 76.5 grains	3,042 – 3,272
.300 WSM	65.5 – 69.5 grains	3,015 – 3,242

NOTE: Only displayed for comparison purposes, these have not been tested nor are they recommended in any way by the Boone and Crockett Club. Do not use any information in this book in reloading processes.

The question is whether this small gain in recoil is worth the couple hundred extra foot pounds of downrange energy to the user. Only time will tell, but as I see this caliber appear on more and more trophy entries, I think the .300 WSM is here to stay and make quite an impact on the modern hunting world.

This brings in the question of a few other newer calibers and how they stack up. First, let's examine the .25-caliber bullets. With classics like the Savage, the .257 Roberts, and the .25-06, these bullets are well accommodated in available chamberings. This, combined with an overall feeling that the .25-caliber bullet may not be big enough for deer probably led to the failure of the .25 WSSM. Pushing a 100-grain bullet at around 3,200 fps with a charge commonly in the 40-grain range, this bullet is more than adequate out to 350 to 400 yards on a whitetail. Unfortunately now it's only available in very limited offerings and has only been listed once or twice for any entries (those were pronghorn) into Boone and Crockett.

While not quite as popular as the .300 WSM, the .270 WSM has appeared on several trophy entries. This casing allows for quite a bit more powder but the 10 or so extra grains of powder usually only adds 150-180 pounds of downrange energy for max-loaded cartridges. The .270 WSM is listed as the harvest caliber in 25 deer entries.

The final new class of cartridge falls along the same lines as these other short magnum offerings—the .325 WSM and .338 Federal with the .325 WSM being a .323-diameter bullet and the only other common chambering with that diameter being the rare 8mms. It is surprising we have seen any of these at all, but they are showing up on occasional trophy entries; we have five whitetails taken with the .325 WSM. Perhaps with gaining popularity, bullet choice for this caliber may expand, and along with it, the numbers we see coming in—though I have a feeling this caliber will go down in the history books as a failure as well. The .338 Federal

BONUS CHART: DATE OF HARVEST

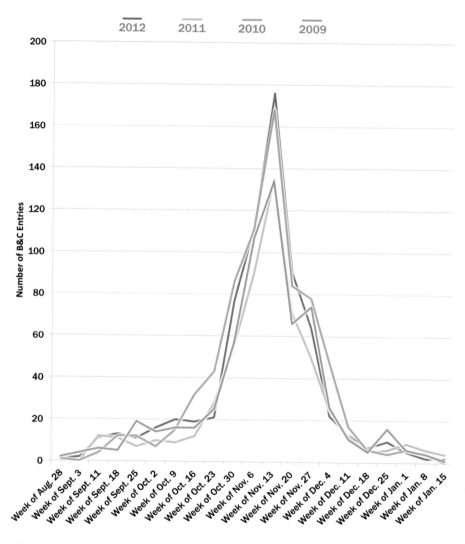

This graph charts the entry rates across the entire country by week killed for nearly 5,500 whitetail deer. The data includes typical and non-typical combined whitetail entries from 2009 through 2012, as well as all methods of take (archery, crossbow, shotgun, rifle, etc.). No picked-up entries are included.

Looking at different calibers, it comes as no surprise that the .300 WSM has surged toward the top of the lists in numerous categories. In 2010 Mickey W. Hellickson harvested this typical buck in Texas with a .300 WSM. It scores 170-7/8 points.

with ample bullet choices does seem to be showing up more commonly in our records, though generally with larger game. I am starting to see a few whitetails taken with this backed-down .338 though.

One final thought I have is I am always surprised with the lack of handgun-taken trophies. With calibers such as the .44 Magnum pushing 240-grain bullets at over 1,400 fps, close-range shots should be more than doable in the hands of a practiced handgunner. Its energy is right at the needed amount to kill a deer. If we look at the big guns, the .454 Casull pushes a 240-grain bullet at over 1,800 fps and the .460 Smith and Wesson pushes a 200-grain FTX bullet out over 2,200 fps. That translates to enough downrange energy to kill a buck at 150 yards.

While the above information makes for great conversation, the basic answer to what is your best whitetail caliber comes down to what you can shoot the most comfortably, can easily get ammunition for, and be proud to carry into camp.

I hope you have enjoyed reviewing these insightful statistics. As the Boone and Crockett Club Records Department continues to gather this detailed data for our records entries on weather, shot conditions, methods of take, etc., we will be able to provide a more complete and intriguing analysis to hunters.

METHOD OF TAKE: OVERVIEW

The pie chart below—demonstrating method of take—shows the breakdown of the different categories that we track. As you can see, nearly half of the entries are taken with a rifle. The archery category includes both traditional and compound bows. We are currently tracking more detailed archery information, but there is not yet enough data to make an accurate assessment.

METHOD	# TROPHY ENTRIES
Rifle	2,543
Archery	1,317
Shotgun	1,021
Muzzleloader	485
Crossbow	181
Handgun	39

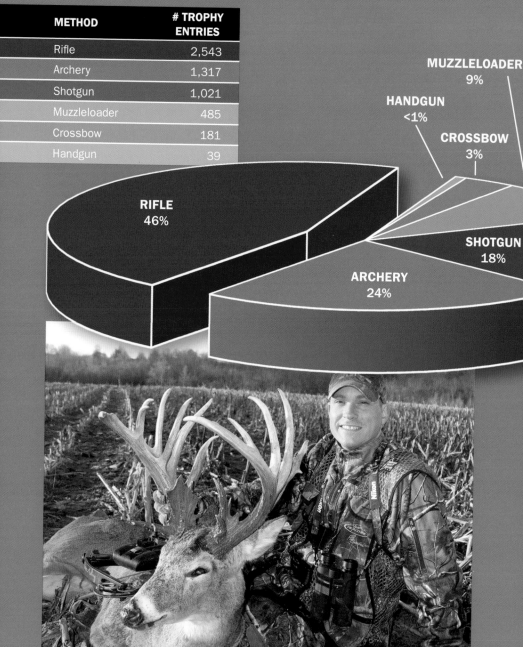

MUZZLELOADER
9%

HANDGUN
<1%

CROSSBOW
3%

RIFLE
46%

SHOTGUN
18%

ARCHERY
24%

ARCHERY (compound) – Ryan K. Welch | non-typical | Kansas | 2012 | 194-3/8 points

SHOTGUN (12 ga.) – Michael L. Burgdorf | typical | Minnesota | 2012 | 193-1/8 points

METHOD OF TAKE: BULLET DIAMETER

Bullets from the .308 diameter class are far and away the most common for harvesting trophy whitetail deer. This graph is based on the data of more than 2,500 whitetail deer entries.

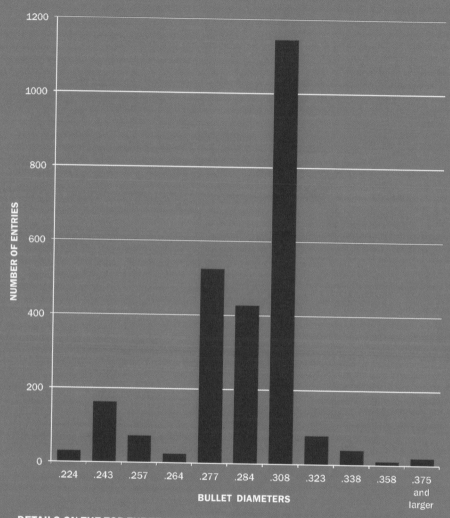

DETAILS ON THE TOP-THREE DIAMETERS

The .277 category is dominated by the .270 Winchester.

The .284 is mostly made up of the 7mm Mags and a few 7mm-08s.

The most common calibers we see for the .308 diameter bullets are .30-06; .300 Win. Mag., .300 WSM, .30-30 Winchester, and .300 Weatherby, which all fall in the top individual caliber choices, as shown on page 230.

.308 CLASS (.300 Win. Mag.) – Cayce W. Bennett | typical
Nebraska | 2013 | 174-5/8 points

.277 CLASS (.270 Win.) – Bernie L. Goebel | typical
Ontario | 2010 | 160-2/8 points

METHOD OF TAKE: CALIBERS

CALIBER	# OF TROPHIES TAKEN
.30-06 Springfield	596
.270 Winchester	485
7mm Rem. Mag	314
.300 Win. Mag	205
.243/6mm	145
.308 Winchester	137
.30-30	84
.300 WSM	78
.25-06	52
.300 Weatherby	52

This graph delves into the high-end detail of the rifle specifics highlighting the top-10 calibers used when harvesting a B&C trophy whitetail.

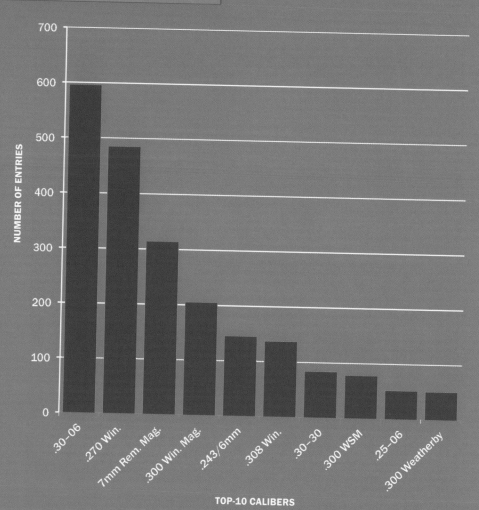

.30-06 SPRINGFIELD – James A. Pike | non-typical | Alberta | 2010 | 196 points

7MM REM. MAG. – Richard G. Wydoski | typical | Kansas | 2012 | 163-5/8 points

Reference Section

Whitetail Records and Distribution

Current B&C Records and Distribution

THE FOLLOWING TABLES RANK ALL THE STATES AND PROVINC-
es that have a typical or non-typical whitetail entry recorded in the
Club's North American Big Game Records Program. The minimum
entry score for typical whitetail is 160 points, and 185 points for
non-typical whitetail deer. The data used in the Table 1 dates back
to 1800s up through December 31, 2013. The oldest whitetail on
file was taken by Arthur Young in McKean County, Pennsylvania,
in 1830.

In Table 2, we've narrowed down the dates to the last ten years with
only deer entered between 2004-2013 included in the dataset. From that
current state/province list we generated Tables 3-7 with detailed county list
and state maps for the top 5 states.

Table 1.
Historic State/Province List for Whitetail Deer from 1830-2013.

State/Province	No. of Whitetail Entries Typical and Non-typical Combined	Rank
Wisconsin	1468	1
Illinois	1286	2
Iowa	1139	3
Minnesota	1012	4
Kentucky	796	5
Saskatchewan	768	6
Ohio	747	7
Missouri	704	8
Kansas	661	9
Texas	597	10
Indiana	549	11
Alberta	522	12
Nebraska	295	13
Michigan	243	14
Georgia	211	15
Oklahoma	196	16

State/Province	No. of Whitetail Entries Typical and Non-typical Combined	Rank
Arkansas	190	17
South Dakota	163	18
Maine	149	19
Mississippi	144	20
Montana	144	20
Manitoba	136	22
Virginia	132	23
New York	107	24
North Dakota	105	25
Ontario	98	26
Maryland	92	27
Idaho	91	28
Pennsylvania	83	29
British Columbia	76	30
Louisiana	76	30
Washington	61	32
Colorado	58	33
Tennessee	57	34
New Hampshire	52	35
Unknown	47	36
Mexico	43	37
Wyoming	37	38
New Brunswick	36	39
Alabama	31	40
North Carolina	31	40
West Virginia	28	42
Delaware	26	43
Quebec	24	44
Massachusetts	23	45
Nova Scotia	23	45
Connecticut	19	47
Vermont	17	48
South Carolina	12	49
New Jersey	10	50
Oregon	7	51
Rhode Island	4	52
Florida	2	53
New Mexico	1	54

Table 2.
Current State/Province List for Whitetail Deer from 2004-2013.

State/Province	No. of Whitetail Entries Typical and Non-typical Combined	Rank
Wisconsin	756	1
Illinois	576	2
Kentucky	432	3
Iowa	430	4
Ohio	427	5
Missouri	361	6
Indiana	353	7
Kansas	333	8
Minnesota	333	8
Saskatchewan	266	10
Texas	225	11
Alberta	197	12
Nebraska	135	13
Oklahoma	87	14
Mississippi	70	15
Michigan	66	16
Arkansas	63	17
South Dakota	59	18
Ontario	58	19
North Dakota	53	20
Georgia	50	21
Pennsylvania	43	22
New York	39	23
Virginia	39	23
British Columbia	37	25
Maryland	36	26
Maine	32	27
Idaho	29	28
Colorado	25	29
Tennessee	25	29
Montana	22	31
Manitoba	20	32
Quebec	19	33
Massachusetts	15	34
Louisiana	13	35

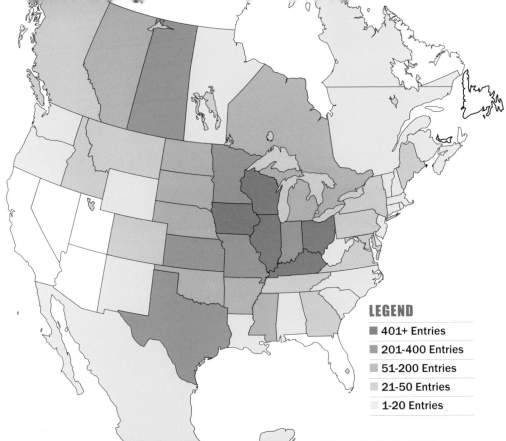

LEGEND
- ■ 401+ Entries
- ■ 201-400 Entries
- ■ 51-200 Entries
- ■ 21-50 Entries
- ■ 1-20 Entries

State/Province	No. of Whitetail Entries Typical and Non-typical Combined	Rank
New Hampshire	13	35
Vermont	13	35
Delaware	12	38
Washington	12	38
North Carolina	11	40
Connecticut	9	42
West Virginia	9	42
Alabama	8	44
Mexico	8	44
New Brunswick	5	46
South Carolina	5	46
Wyoming	5	46
New Jersey	4	49
Nova Scotia	3	50
Rhode Island	3	50
New Mexico	1	52
Oregon	1	52

In the following tables we drilled down into the data for the current (2004-2013) top five states to provide detailed information about the counties in those states.

Table 3.
County Breakdown for Wisconsin
Combined Whitetail Deer Entries from 2004-2013

County	Whitetail Entries Typical and Non-typical Combined	County continued...	Whitetail Entries Typical and Non-typical Combined
Buffalo	55	Jefferson	9
Trempealeau	32	Sheboygan	9
Sauk	29	Walworth	9
Waupaca	27	Winnebago	9
Shawano	26	Clark	8
Grant	23	Oconto	8
Vernon	23	Sawyer	8
Dunn	22	Washington	8
Richland	22	Waushara	8
Crawford	21	Burnett	7
Pierce	20	Fond du Lac	7
Dane	19	Manitowoc	7
Columbia	17	Rock	7
Dodge	16	Rusk	7
Marathon	16	Wood	7
Polk	16	Bayfield	6
Pepin	15	Door	6
Marquette	14	Green Lake	6
Outagamie	13	Langlade	6
Chippewa	12	St. Croix	6
Jackson	12	Waukesha	6
Green	11	Lincoln	5
Iowa	11	Oneida	5
Juneau	11	Taylor	5
Barron	10	Washburn	5
Eau Claire	10	Brown	4
La Crosse	10	Lafayette	4
Monroe	10	Marinette	4
Adams	9	Racine	4
Douglas	9	Iron	3

WISCONSIN

County continued...	Whitetail Entries Typical and Non-typical Combined
Kewaunee	3
Portage	3
Price	3
Calumet	2
Forest	2
Kenosha	2
Menominee	2
Milwaukee	2
Ashland	1
Ozaukee	1

LEGEND

- ■ 50+ Entries
- ■ 20-49 Entries
- ■ 10-19 Entries
- ■ 5-9 Entries
- □ 1-4 Entries

Table 4.
County Breakdown for Illinois Combined Whitetail Deer Entries from 2004-2013.

County	Whitetail Entries Typical and Non-typical Combined	County continued...	Whitetail Entries Typical and Non-typical Combined
Pike	24	Warren	6
Fulton	23	Wayne	6
Adams	22	Woodford	6
Jo Daviess	21	Henry	5
Hancock	17	Livingston	5
Macoupin	16	Madison	5
Schuyler	16	Mason	5
Greene	15	Stephenson	5
Randolph	15	Will	5
Clark	13	Coles	4
Knox	13	Crawford	4
Brown	12	Cumberland	4
Peoria	12	Edwards	4
Bureau	11	Gallatin	4
Morgan	11	Hamilton	4
Iroquois	9	Henderson	4
Jasper	9	La Salle	4
Sangamon	9	Lee	4
Shelby	9	McHenry	4
White	9	Menard	4
Calhoun	8	Montgomery	4
Edgar	8	Richland	4
Fayette	8	Tazewell	4
McLean	8	Union	4
St. Clair	8	Washington	4
Jersey	7	Williamson	4
Marshall	7	Bond	3
Perry	7	Clinton	3
Cass	6	Franklin	3
Christian	6	Jackson	3
Mercer	6	Jefferson	3
Rock Island	6	Kankakee	3
Vermilion	6	Kendall	3

ILLINOIS

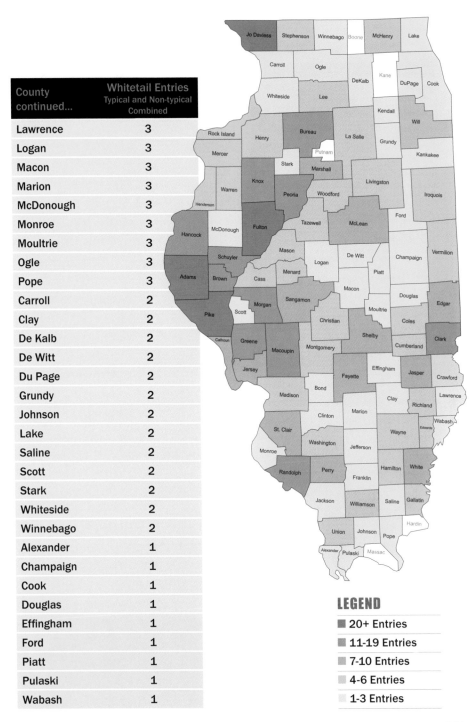

County continued...	Whitetail Entries Typical and Non-typical Combined
Lawrence	3
Logan	3
Macon	3
Marion	3
McDonough	3
Monroe	3
Moultrie	3
Ogle	3
Pope	3
Carroll	2
Clay	2
De Kalb	2
De Witt	2
Du Page	2
Grundy	2
Johnson	2
Lake	2
Saline	2
Scott	2
Stark	2
Whiteside	2
Winnebago	2
Alexander	1
Champaign	1
Cook	1
Douglas	1
Effingham	1
Ford	1
Piatt	1
Pulaski	1
Wabash	1

LEGEND
- 20+ Entries
- 11-19 Entries
- 7-10 Entries
- 4-6 Entries
- 1-3 Entries

Table 5.
County Breakdown for Kentucky Combined Whitetail Deer Entries from 2004-2013.

County	Whitetail Entries Typical and Non-typical Combined	County continued...	Whitetail Entries Typical and Non-typical Combined
Lewis	14	Barren	4
Casey	12	Bracken	4
Hardin	12	Breathitt	4
Christian	11	Carter	4
Grayson	11	Estill	4
Henry	11	Franklin	4
Logan	11	Gallatin	4
Ohio	10	Green	4
Butler	9	Jefferson	4
Hopkins	9	Jessamine	4
Pulaski	9	Leslie	4
Whitley	9	Marion	4
Breckinridge	8	McLean	4
Hart	8	Metcalfe	4
Henderson	8	Muhlenberg	4
Pendleton	8	Russell	4
Trigg	8	Woodford	4
Edmonson	6	Adair	3
Fayette	6	Ballard	3
Garrard	6	Campbell	3
Greenup	6	Carlisle	3
Madison	6	Carroll	3
Todd	6	Clay	3
Boone	5	Daviess	3
Caldwell	5	Graves	3
Crittenden	5	Harlan	3
Harrison	5	Knox	3
Kenton	5	Livingston	3
Oldham	5	Nelson	3
Owen	5	Pike	3
Shelby	5	Robertson	3
Trimble	5	Rockcastle	3
Union	5	Scott	3

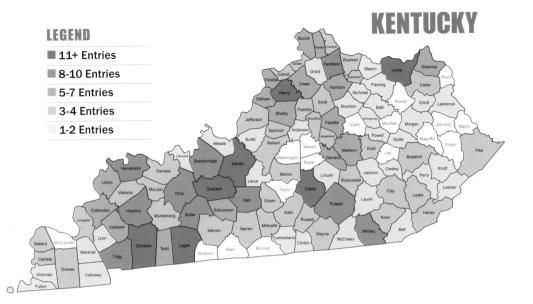

LEGEND

- ■ 11+ Entries
- ■ 8-10 Entries
- ■ 5-7 Entries
- ■ 3-4 Entries
- ■ 1-2 Entries

KENTUCKY

County continued...	Whitetail Entries Typical and Non-typical Combined
Spencer	3
Warren	3
Webster	3
Bath	2
Bell	2
Clinton	2
Elliott	2
Fleming	2
Fulton	2
Grant	2
Jackson	2
Laurel	2
Mason	2
McCreary	2
Meade	2
Montgomery	2
Morgan	2
Nicholas	2
Owsley	2
Perry	2
Powell	2

County continued...	Whitetail Entries Typical and Non-typical Combined
Wayne	2
Anderson	1
Bourbon	1
Bullitt	1
Calloway	1
Cumberland	1
Hancock	1
Hickman	1
Knott	1
Larue	1
Lawrence	1
Letcher	1
Lincoln	1
Lyon	1
Marshall	1
Wolfe	1

Table 6.
County Breakdown for Iowa
Combined Whitetail Deer Entries from 2004-2013.

County	Whitetail Entries Typical and Non-typical Combined	County continued...	Whitetail Entries Typical and Non-typical Combined
Dubuque	22	Boone	4
Van Buren	22	Buchanan	4
Allamakee	21	Clarke	4
Clayton	19	Clinton	4
Monroe	17	Delaware	4
Decatur	15	Iowa	4
Jackson	14	Johnson	4
Warren	14	Lee	4
Lucas	13	Mills	4
Davis	11	Pottawattamie	4
Madison	11	Scott	4
Harrison	10	Story	4
Union	10	Webster	4
Des Moines	9	Woodbury	4
Linn	9	Butler	3
Fremont	8	Chickasaw	3
Guthrie	8	Floyd	3
Marion	8	Page	3
Polk	8	Adams	2
Taylor	8	Hardin	2
Wayne	7	Henry	2
Fayette	6	Mahaska	2
Keokuk	6	Marshall	2
Muscatine	6	Plymouth	2
Ringgold	6	Sioux	2
Benton	5	Washington	2
Dallas	5	Audubon	1
Jefferson	5	Bremer	1
Jones	5	Carroll	1
Monona	5	Cass	1
Montgomery	5	Cedar	1
Wapello	5	Cerro Gordo	1
Winneshiek	5	Crawford	1
Appanoose	4	Hamilton	1

IOWA

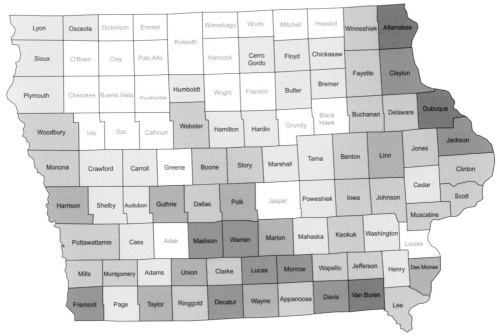

LEGEND

- 20+ Entries
- 11-19 Entries
- 7-10 Entries
- 4-6 Entries
- 1-3 Entries

Table 7.
County Breakdown for Ohio
Combined Whitetail Deer Entries from 2004-2013.

County	Whitetail Entries Typical and Non-typical Combined	County continued...	Whitetail Entries Typical and Non-typical Combined
Highland	19	Richland	5
Licking	19	Stark	5
Coshocton	16	Summit	5
Adams	12	Washington	5
Ross	12	Clark	4
Warren	12	Clermont	4
Carroll	11	Darke	4
Logan	11	Geauga	4
Delaware	10	Hocking	4
Fairfield	10	Jefferson	4
Franklin	10	Mahoning	4
Portage	10	Meigs	4
Greene	9	Pickaway	4
Pike	9	Shelby	4
Butler	8	Vinton	4
Noble	8	Wayne	4
Tuscarawas	8	Wood	4
Ashtabula	7	Athens	3
Auglaize	7	Medina	3
Guernsey	7	Monroe	3
Hamilton	7	Morgan	3
Ashland	6	Morrow	3
Belmont	6	Preble	3
Brown	6	Sandusky	3
Champaign	6	Trumbull	3
Miami	6	Williams	3
Muskingum	6	Allen	2
Scioto	6	Columbiana	2
Clinton	5	Crawford	2
Erie	5	Cuyahoga	2
Holmes	5	Fulton	2
Lorain	5	Gallia	2
Perry	5	Hardin	2

OHIO

LEGEND
- ■ 17+ Entries
- ■ 11-16 Entries
- ■ 7-10 Entries
- ■ 4-6 Entries
- ■ 1-3 Entries

County continued...	Whitetail Entries Typical and Non-typical Combined
Harrison	2
Huron	2
Knox	2
Lawrence	2
Lucas	2
Ottawa	2
Paulding	2
Van Wert	2
Fayette	1

County continued...	Whitetail Entries Typical and Non-typical Combined
Henry	1
Jackson	1
Lake	1
Madison	1
Marion	1
Montgomery	1
Seneca	1
Wyandot	1

Table 8.
Top 15 Typical Whitetail Deer
Hunter-Taken between 2004-2013

Final Score	Main Beam (left)	Main Beam (right)	Inside Spread	No. of Points (left)	No. of Points (right)	Location	Hunter(s)	Date	Rank
202-3/8	28-1/8	27-5/8	28-6/8	10	7	N. Saskatchewan River, SK	J. Tarala & M. Berezowski	2006	*
201-1/8	29	29-6/8	24-1/8	5	6	Warren Co., OH	Bradley S. Jerman	2004	11
200-1/8	26-5/8	26-3/8	18-7/8	7	7	Otauwau River, AB	Eugene I. Kurinka	2005	*
198-6/8	27-1/8	28-5/8	20-1/8	8	9	White Co., IL	Joseph B. Girten	2006	22
198-3/8	25-2/8	26	21-7/8	6	6	Good Spirit Lake, SK	Blaine D. Kreps	2005	25
198-3/8	26	26-7/8	19-4/8	7	7	Muskingum Co., OH	Timothy E. Reed	2004	25
198-2/8	24-6/8	26-7/8	21-1/8	8	9	Saunders Co., NE	Kevin S. Petrzilka	2010	28
198-1/8	30-4/8	31-1/8	20-7/8	5	5	Greene Co., IL	Charles Q. Rives	2006	30
196-6/8	27-6/8	29-6/8	19-5/8	7	5	Adams Co., OH	Justin L. Metzner	2006	*
196-3/8	26-1/8	25-7/8	23-1/8	5	5	Fulton Co., IL	Roger H. Mann	2004	43
194-3/8	28-1/8	29-3/8	19-5/8	5	5	Montgomery Co., IA	Mark A. Lewis	2008	*
193-2/8	27-3/8	27-1/8	15-2/8	7	7	Harper Co., KS	Keith J. Manca	2007	*
193-1/8	27-7/8	28-2/8	22	7	7	Winona Co., MN	Michael L. Burgdorf	2012	74
192-6/8	28-7/8	29-2/8	26-3/8	8	7	Taylor Co., IA	Terry L. Lundquist	2009	*
192-5/8	29-4/8	30-5/8	20-1/8	12	9	Pushmataha Co., OK	Jason L. Boyett	2007	83

* Final score subject to verification by Awards Judges Panel or additional verifying measurements.

Kevin S. Petrzilka

Michael L. Burgdorf

Keith J. Manca

Jason L. Boyett

Justin L. Metzner

Eugene I. Kurinka

Bradley S. Jerman

Table 9.
Top 15 Non-Typical Whitetail Deer
Hunter-Taken between 2004-2013

Final Score	Main Beam (left)	Main Beam (right)	Inside Spread	No. of Points (left)	No. of Points (right)	Location	Hunter(s)	Date	Rank
305-7/8	29-6/8	30-4/8	23-6/8	21	16	Huntington Co., IN	Timothy J. Beck	2012	5
295-3/8	24-5/8	21-6/8	18-4/8	22	25	McDonough Co., IL	Scott R. Dexter	2004	8
295-3/8	29	30-2/8	25-1/8	17	18	Adams Co., OH	Jonathan R. Schmucker	2006	8
293-3/8	27-5/8	30	18-7/8	21	22	Dallas Co., IA	Tim A. Forret	2012	11
284	24-2/8	22-2/8	16-1/8	14	22	Richardson Co., NE	Wesley A. O'Brien	2009	13
278-2/8	25-2/8	25-7/8	22-2/8	18	17	Harrison Co., IA	Ryan M. Stolz	2012	19
275-5/8	27-1/8	26-1/8	24	15	13	Jackson Co., IA	Kyle M. Simmons	2008	22
274	22-4/8	19-1/8	27-7/8	20	16	Cross Lake, AB	Helgie H. Eymundson	2007	23
272-2/8	27-6/8	27-4/8	23-2/8	13	14	Morris Co., KS	Gerald E. Rightmyer	2006	26
268-4/8	20-2/8	18-7/8	20-1/8	19	12	Houston Co., TX	Mark E. Lee	2013	30
268-1/8	25-6/8	25-7/8	20-6/8	14	14	Charles Co., MD	William D. Crutchfield, Jr.	2006	*
260-6/8	25-1/8	26-4/8	21-6/8	17	10	N. Saskatchewan River, SK	Maverick Windels	2011	*
257-4/8	25-7/8	26-4/8	19-6/8	10	14	Summit Co., OH	Jeffery T. McCulley	2010	*
256-4/8	19-4/8	17-3/8	19-7/8	13	15	San Jacinto Co., TX	AJ J. Downs	2012	60
256-3/8	25-7/8	25-5/8	20-5/8	10	12	Marshall Co., IL	Steve Wallis	200	61

* Final score subject to verification by Awards Judges Panel or additional verifying measurements.

Scott R. Dexter

Mark E. Lee

Gerald E. Rightmyer

Kyle M. Simmons

William D. Crutchfield, Jr.

Timothy J. Beck

Helgie H. Eymundson

Field Photo Tips

FIELD PHOTOGRAPHY IS AN IMPORTANT PART OF ANY HUNT, whether it's your first-ever harvest, which may be a doe, or it's the buck you've been tracking season after season. It will undoubtedly be shown to friends and acquaintances when you relive the tale of your hunt. It may also be around for future generations in your family to see what hunting "back in the day" was like, what clothes you wore, the habitat you were hunting, and which rifle you were shooting.

The following pages offer a few tips and examples that will help you the next time you're in the field after a successful day. Each issue of *Fair Chase* magazine includes dozens of top-notch field photographs including tips to consider when taking your field photos. Join B&C's Associates Program to receive the magazine or visit B&C's web site (www.boone-crockett.org) for even more tips and suggestions.

TRAPS TO AVOID

- Do not sit on your deer. Make sure the animal is positioned in a respectful manner.

- Do not take your photo in the back of a truck or vehicle.

- Be mindful of the direction of your firearm. The barrel should always be pointed in a safe direction, not at the hunter or anyone else in the photo or area.

- Take a look at what is behind you before you take the picture. Make sure there aren't any gut piles, bloody grass or snow, vehicles, etc.

- Make sure your digital settings are for a high-quality photograph, not low resolution.

- If the hunter is wearing a ball cap, make sure it's not casting a dark shadow on their face. If it is, 1) remove the cap, 2) tip it back to reduce the cast of the shadow, or 3) use the fill flash on your camera.

FIELD PHOTO TIP: Take Advantage of the Sky

Sky is a field photographer's best friend, especially blue sky. By sky-lining your deer's antlers you accomplish two things. For one, you will capture a clear account of the trophy quality of your animal. Secondly, by consciously putting blue sky in the background you will also avoid the tendency to sit right behind your deer's antler, erasing any benefit of taking the time to skyline its rack.

Consider sitting to the side and slightly behind your buck with its head tipped forward instead of level or nose tipped up. This is the best head position for a tall racked buck.

Hoyt A. Childs III – Typical whitetail, 2011, Kansas, 171-2/8 points

Lucas T. Cochren – Non-typical whitetail, Kansas, 238-4/8 points

The next time big sky is available, try positioning your trophy to take full advantage.

FIELD PHOTO TIP: Additional People

The one-on-one quest of man versus prey and the elements are what we associate with hunting, but this is not always the case. Family and friends can and often do join in the action, especially if a young hunter is involved or the hunt takes place in rough country where there is safety in numbers.

Field photos with more than one person can therefore present a composition challenge, but one that is easily overcome with a little extra effort. Naturally, the animal should be the focal point. To answer the question for the observer who the hunter is, the person who harvested the deer should be the one closest to and holding the buck. If there are more than two people in the photo, they should be evenly distributed around the animal and the hunter, with as much equal billing as possible. Typically lost in these group shots is any background of the location from trying to make room in the frame for everyone.

Charles R. DeWitt – Typical whitetail, Missouri, 2003, 230-6/8 points

Cole G. Medlin – Typical whitetail, Texas, 2009, 180-1/8 points

FIELD PHOTO TIP: Look at the Camera... or Don't

Look at the camera. Smile. It's a natural response. You're here with your trophy. The cameras' over there. Where do we always look? At the camera.

The straight on, looking at the birdie, pose is certainly a mandatory shot to take. One we can do without even thinking. But while you're at it try looking admiringly at your trophy for a few takes. You might be surprised which photo will stand out as not only being different than all the rest, but it might just be the one showing you and your trophy's "best side."

Joseph C. June, Jr. – Typical whitetail, 2011, Illinois, 162-7/8 points

Go ahead take the mandatory straight-on photo, put take a few while you're looking at your deer too.

FIELD PHOTO TIP: Assets Forward

Face it, we look at field photos from an "antler/horn first" perspective. We're hunters, this is what appeals to the eye first, over scenery and smiles, composition and lighting. That said, every trophy has its strong points and these assets should be brought forward. All of the whitetail deer shown here have very unique non-typical characteristics, which may not have been apparent from a straight-on angle.

Bottom line... take photos from multiple angles.

Brian M. Stephens – Non-typical whitetail, Ohio, 2009, 232-5/8 points

Justin S. Smith – Non-typical whitetail, Wisconsin, 2012, 197-4/8 points

Robert G. Senecal – Non-typical whitetail, Alberta, 2011, 213-4/8 points

Brad C. Dobbs – Non-typical whitetail, Colorado, 2010, 188-1/8 points

FIELD PHOTO TIP: Memories

Field photos are intended to be memories of the hunt and the hunted. Beyond the animals taken the country in which they lived and you visited are equally valuable to keep with you past the hunt.

Consider removing your hunting gear and equipment in a couple of the photos, which will add to the natural setting and not draw the eye away from the memorable background or the animal.

Next time, if you have the ability to include the habitat that produced your harvest, take the time to include it in the photograph with your trophy. You will not regret the added memory.

Ryan K. Welch – Non-typical whitetail, Kansas, 2012, 194-3/8 points

Doak D. Brown – Typical whitetail, Texas, 2013, 172-5/8 points

Consider including the habitat as well as your firearm/bow in the photo to help retain memories of your successful hunt.

FIELD PHOTO TIP: Ol' Reliable

Black Smoke, The Closer, Auto 5, The Heater, Hog Leg. Giving nicknames to our favorite hunting instrument dates back even before Fess Parker, Davy Crockett and Ole' Betsy. But what of field photography with Ol' Reliable? Is there an appropriate way to display your trusty companion and your trophy in a field photo?

Given everything on our minds at the time, this minor detail may be why we all have seen images either showed a disrespect for the animal, unsafe positioning of a firearm, barrels in front of faces, or ones that dominated the photo as to say, "Here's my rifle/ bow and the critter I got." Truth is, your gun or bow was an important part of the hunt and the memory. Posing with them is therefore a natural. Here a few suggestions.

Safety is always job one. In the heat of the moment, double check to make sure your firearm is unloaded and pointed in a safe direction for the photo taking. In days gone by putting a rifle between the antlers of a trophy must have been considered a yardstick of accomplishment of sorts. These poses seem to have fallen by the wayside in recent times. Laying you gun or bow on the animal is certainly more appealing, but simply holding your rifle or bow behind the animal tends to make for the best composed, safest and most respectful field photos. If you chose this, the last thing to check for is making sure you weapon is at your side making you and your trophy the focal points of the photograph.

Jody D. Beauchane ~ Typical whitetail, Minnesota, 2012, 163-4/8 points

Suggested Reading

HUNTING AND SHOOTING

Boddington, Craig (1997). *American Hunting Rifles: Their Application in the Field for Practical Shooting.* California: Safari Press.

Boddington, Craig (1999). *Make It Accurate: Get the Maximum Performance From Your Hunting Rifle.* California: Safari Press.

Boddington, Craig (2005). *The Perfect Shot, North America: Shot Placement for North American Big Game.* California: Safari Press.

Boddington, Craig (1997). *Shots at Big Game.* California: Safari Press.

Koller, Larry (2000, 1970, 1948). *Shots at Whitetails.* Wisconsin: Krause Publications.

Kroll, J. & Whittington, G. (1994). *The Art and Science of Patterning Whitetails.* Texas: Center of Applied Studies of Forestry.

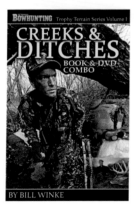

Van Zwoll, Wayne (2004). *The Hunter's Guide to Accurate Shooting: How to Hit What You're Aiming at in Any Situation.* Connecticut: Lyon's Press.

Winke, Bill (2009). *Setting Up the Perfect Hunting Bow.* Florida: Petersen's Bowhunting.

Winke, Bill (2013). *Trophy Terrain: Creeks & Ditches Book & DVD Combo.* Florida: Petersen's Bowhunting.

Wootters, John (1997). *Hunting Trophy Deer.* Connecticut: Lyons Press.

MANAGEMENT

Cain III, J.W. & Krausman, P.R. (Eds.) (2013*). Wildlife Management and Conservation: Contemporary Principles and Practices.* Maryland: Johns Hopkins University Press

Fulbright, T.E. & Ortega-Santos, J.A. (2013). *White-Tailed Deer Habitat: Ecology and Management on Rangelands (Perspectives on South Texas, sponsored by Texas A&M University-Kingsville).* Texas: Texas A&M University Press.

Heffelfinger, James (2006). *Deer of the Southwest.* Texas: Texas A&M University Press.

Hewitt, David G. (2011). *Biology and Management of White-tailed Deer.* Texas: CRC Press.

Krausman, P.R. & Leopold, B.D. (Eds.) (2013). *Essential Readings in Wildlife Management and Conservation.* Maryland: Johns Hopkins University Press

Richards, D. & Brothers, A. (2003). *Observing & Evaluating Whitetails.* Texas: Self published.

WEB RESOURCES

Boone and Crockett Club
  www.boone-crockett.org

Field & Stream > Blogs > Whitetail 365
  www.fieldandstream.com/blogs/whitetail-365

Growing Deer TV
  www.growingdeer.tv

Midwest Whitetail
  www.MidwestWhitetail.com

North American Whitetail
  www.northamericanwhitetail.com

Outdoor Life > Hunting > Whitetail Deer
  www.outdoorlife.com/hunting/whitetail-deer

Quality Deer Management Association
  www.qdma.com

Wildlife and Hunting Organizations

Following is the complete list of wildlife and hunting organizations that make up the American Wildlife Conservation Partners (AWCP), which was founded by Boone and Crockett Club in 2000. Since then AWCP has leveraged the strength of 6 million hunter-conservationists to advance the interests of wildlife, habitat, and hunting heritage.

The AWCP envisions a future in which,

...all wildlife and private and public habitats are abundant, maintained, and enhanced;

...hunting, trapping, and other outdoor interests are supported by the public to maintain America's great wildlife conservation heritage and cultural traditions;

...natural resources policies encourage, empower, and reward stewardship and responsible use;

...all people are committed to principles of scientific wildlife management, where wildlife is held in public trust, and where the use of resources is shared equitably and sustained for present and future generations.

AWCP ORGANIZATIONS

- Archery Trade Association
- Association of Fish & Wildlife Agencies
- Bear Trust International
- Boone and Crockett Club
- Bowhunting Preservation Alliance
- Buckmasters American Deer Foundation
- Camp Fire Club of America
- Catch A Dream Foundation
- Congressional Sportsmen's Foundation
- Conservation Force
- The Conservation Fund
- Dallas Safari Club
- Delta Waterfowl Foundation
- Ducks Unlimited

- Houston Safari Club
- International Hunter Education Association
- Izaak Walton League of America
- Masters of Foxhounds Foundation
- Mule Deer Foundation
- National Association of Forest Service Retirees
- National Rifle Association of America
- National Shooting Sports Foundation
- National Trappers Association
- National Wild Turkey Federation
- North American Bear Foundation
- North American Grouse Partnership
- Orion The Hunter's Institute
- Pheasants Forever
- Pope and Young Club
- Public Lands Foundation
- Quail Forever
- Quality Deer Management Association
- Rocky Mountain Elk Foundation
- Ruffed Grouse Society
- Safari Club International
- Sand County Foundation
- Shikar Safari Club
- Texas Wildlife Association
- The Wildlife Society
- Theodore Roosevelt Conservation Partnership
- Tread Lightly!
- U. S. Sportsmen's Alliance
- Whitetails Unlimited
- Wild Sheep Foundation
- Wildlife Forever
- Wildlife Habitat Council
- Wildlife Management Institute
- Wildlife Mississippi

About the Authors

RENÉ BARRIENTOS

René was raised in Eagle Pass, Maverick County, Texas, one of the top whitetail-producing counties in Texas back when leases were rare and hunting opportunities abounded. This spawned a devotion to hunting any available game, taking his first deer at age 10. He set his goals from following *Outdoor Life* and *Field and Stream* and fulfilled them with hunting many of North American big game species.

René has harvested 10 whitetail bucks that qualify for Boone and Crockett Club's All-time Big Game Records book. He graduated from the University of Texas School of Law in 1978 and was a civil litigator until retiring in 2010, all the while operating a ranch in South Texas. He was previously recognized as the Statewide Lone Star Land Steward for his conservation and management practices on his ranch. René is a regular member of the Boone and Crockett Club.

CRAIG BODDINGTON

Craig Boddington is one of America's most prolific outdoor writers, with more than 4000 published articles and 25 books on hunting, firearms, and conservation. Although perhaps best-known for his international hunting, Boddington maintains that he is first and foremost a hunter of our white-tailed deer, a species he has pursued in several dozen U.S. and Mexican states and Canadian provinces. A native of Kansas, Boddington grew up in a time when Kansas had no modern deer season, so blames the whitetail for his hunting wanderlust...but today reckons the height of his year to be hunting whitetails in his native Kansas.

Boddington graduated with an English degree from the University of Kansas and was commissioned in the Unites States Marine Corps. After five years on active duty he joined Petersen Publishing Company in 1979, and from 1981 to 1994 served as Editor of Petersen's HUNTING Magazine. He then managed to escape the Los Angeles office, but has continued to contribute to both Guns & Ammo and Petersen's HUNTING, now serving as Executive Field Editor for InterMedia Outdoors. He continued his military career in the Marine Corps Reserve, retiring in 2005 after 31 years service as an infantry officer. Boddington now divides his time between California's Central Coast and a small farm in southern Kansas. Active in numerous conservation and hunting organizations for many years, he has been a Professional Member of Boone and Crockett since 1983.

RICHARD HALE

Richard received a biology degree from Pittsburgh State University and a dental degree from University of Missouri in 1987. He has hunted on five continents and enjoys many types of hunting.

He attended his first Boone and Crockett meeting in the mid-1980s. As a regular member of the Club since 1994, he has served as an Official Measurer, as well as on the Records of North American Big Game Committee for many years. He served as a panel judge for the 27th and 28th Big Game Awards Programs. Richard has served as co-chairman and was appointed as chairman of the Club's Records of North American Big Game Records Committee in 2013, which he considers a great honor.

Present day activities include teaching his wife Shirley and 17-year-old daughter Abby more than they want to know about management of wild whitetail deer on their eastern Kansas farms. Hunting and guiding others to trophy bucks has been his passion for... too long to mention.

KEN HAYWORTH

Ken Hayworth was born and raised in Hudson Bay, Saskatchewan. He didn't start hunting until he was 20 years old when he was introduced to the whitetail woods by his father-in-law who had just starting a whitetail outfitting business. He spent the next 17 years learning about hunting whitetails and working as a guide. Ken wanted to stay close to the whitetail woods so he never went far from his hometown working at the local OSB mill.

He has since harvested three whitetail bucks that have net scored over 200 non-typical inches and several that have scored over 165 inches. The constant challenge of finding and watching deer grow into mature monsters is what keeps him going back into the woods to pursue whitetail.

JAY LESSER

Jay is a Custom gun builder and a well-known Wyoming outfitter. He has served as a Board member of the Wyoming Outfitters and Guides Association for three terms. In his spare time, Jay also finds time to write articles for several large gun and hunting publications.

JACK RENEAU

Jack Reneau is a certified wildlife biologist who has been Director of Big Game Records for B&C since 1983, a Professional Member since 1986, an Official Measurer since 1976, and a Records Committee member since 1997. Jack earned a MS and BS in Wildlife Management from Eastern Kentucky University and Colorado State University, respectively. Prior to working for B&C, he worked for National Rifle Association where he was involved with trophy processing, the 16th Awards Program Banquet, and the 7th edition of the All-time records book. He has authored/edited over 40 B&C books/publications.

In 1986, Jack was involved with developing the predecessor to Fair Chase magazine, titled Boone and Crockett Club's Associates Newsletter. He was assistant editor for the Associates Newsletter and is assistant editor for Fair Chase. He has written a quarterly column for the Associates Newsletter/Fair Chase titled "Trophy Talk" from 1986 to the present.

Jack has been involved with all aspects of the Club's records program for over 37 years. He was involved with computerizing the trophy data starting in 1976. He was also involved with developing B&C's Official Measurer training workshop program in 1976 that is still used today. He has conducted over 60 measurer training workshops, training most of the Club's current 1,300 measurers. He has been involved with planning/coordinating 12 Big Game Awards Programs. In 1977 he traveled to New York City with Lowell Baier and Harold Nesbitt to salvage remnants of the National Collection of Heads and Horns from the Bronx Zoo.

DAVE RICHARDS

After receiving a Marketing degree from Southeastern Louisiana University Dave Richards began his outdoor career path 28 years ago. He is a manufacturer's representative with H&G Marketing for several leading companies in the hunting and shooting sports. He has won many awards in the outdoor industry including Rep of the Year for both Leupold in 2007 and Nosler in 2002.

A self taught photographer, he began photographing his hunting adventures and the wildlife he encountered and by college was selling images to frame shops and outdoor publications. Since those early years he has traveled from Florida to Alaska pursuing unique images of wildlife from bears to eagles. However, his favorite subject to photograph is mature whitetails. Over the years his images have graced the covers and pages of numerous

outdoor publications, books, and ad campaigns.

In 2003, Observing & Evaluating Whitetails, his book co-authored with biologist Al Brothers was published through Quality Deer Management Assoc. Contained among the books 435 stunning color images are many impressive bucks Dave photographed over multiple years providing a comprehensive overview of how to age and score white-tailed deer through physical characteristics and behavior. A technique he learned from the Roy Hindes family and chronicled while photographing many years on their ranch.

Dave and his wife Beth live with their two sons near Boerne in the Texas hill country.

GLEN SALOW

Glen Salow has a lifelong passion, approaching the state of addiction, with the whitetail deer. Originally from the small rural town of Earlville in Northeast Iowa, he started hunting with his father at a young age and has never stopped. At 14 he arrowed his first P&Y qualifying trophy and has been upping his game ever since. Whether it's scouting, shed hunting

or collecting, or working on different farms and access, Glen's mind is never far from the deer woods.

After attending Kirkwood Community College, Glen found a career in the insurance industry that allows him some flexibility in his schedule. This combined with his beautiful and understanding wife, Ashley Jared, has allowed Glen to follow his passion.

Glen has a total of five Boone and Crockett records-book qualifying deer—one that qualifies for the All-time records book and four that make the Awards book. In an effort to give back to the hunting community Glen attended a Boone and Crockett Official Measurer training workshop in Missoula, Montana, in 2009 and manages to find time to score for both the North American Shed Hunters Club and Boone and Crockett Club.

JUSTIN SPRING

Justin's 9-5 job is as the Assistant Director of Big Game Records for Boone and Crockett Club, but this is purely an extension of his passion for conservation, hunting, and the outdoors. He also writes a regular column for B&C's *Fair Chase* magazine titled, "Beyond the Score" and regularly contributes chapters and records data to B&C publications.

Growing up on the southern Oregon coast, Justin's interest in wildlife was ignited while pursuing Roosevelt's elk, Columbia blacktail deer, and black bear with his father well before he was able to take his first trip afield with a rifle at age 12. He attended college in Northern Wisconsin where he was immersed in the whitetail culture of the upper Midwest. In addition to a degree in wildlife management he moved back out West with his now wife and hunting partner Rebecca. The two of them spend hours meticulously studying draw odds and statistics for locations throughout the U.S. where public land, do-it-yourself pursuit of top-quality trophies is possible.

He and Rebecca make their home in Alberton, Montana, where they base their hunts all over Montana and the rest of the country. Justin has hunted whitetail in five states and has successfully taken bucks with archery, crossbow, and rifle. His passion for the hunt takes him to all corners of the U.S. in pursuit of any species for which he can draw a tag.

LARRY WEISHUHN

A native of Texas, Larry L. Weishuhn, is a wildlife biologist, outdoor writer, book author, television show host, after-dinner speaker, bronze art-

ist, and hunter. He is known throughout the world as "Mr. Whitetail" because of his many years of whitetail deer research, management, hunting and promoting proper habitat and herd management. Larry first became involved in whitetail deer research while still an undergraduate at Texas A&M University working with the Texas' Wildlife Disease Project, with emphasis on antler development, nutrition and management. Later he spent several years as wildlife biologist with the Texas Parks & Wildlife Department before entering the private sector as a wildlife management consultant.

He started hunting whitetail deer with his dad and granddad in south-central Texas while he was still in diapers. Since then he has hunted whitetails extensively in North America and big game throughout the world with rifle and pistol. Hunting has not only been his avocation, but it has also been his vocation. He freely admits, "Every day afield, is a learning experience!"

Larry is Professional Member of Boone and Crockett Club, co-founder of the Texas Wildlife Association, a Life Member of Dallas Safari Club, National Rifle Association and Wild Sheep Foundation. In 2007 he was inducted into the National Legends of the Outdoors Hall of Fame.

BILL WINKE

Bill Winke has been writing full-time for hunting magazines for 23 years. He specializes in articles about hunting strategy—primarily whitetail deer—and assembling, tuning and shooting archery equipment. Bill grew up in Northeast Iowa but has had the amazing opportunity to hunt deer in sixteen states and three Canadian provinces.

In 2008, Bill introduced MidwestWhitetail.com, an online hunting show that has become very popular. In 2010, he produced *Midwest Whitetail TV* for The Sportsman Channel, which won "Best New Series" that year. In 2011, 2012 and 2013, *Midwest Whitetail* won the coveted award of Best Hunting Show on The Sportsman Channel.

Bill earned a degree in mechanical engineering from the University of Iowa in 1986, spent four years working in the aerospace industry in Kalamazoo, Michigan, and now lives on a farm in southern Iowa with his wife Pam, their 15-year-old daughter, Jordan, and their 13-year old son, Drew.

GORDON WHITTINGTON

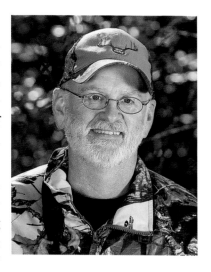

Gordon Whittington has been a full-time staff member of *North American Whitetail* magazine virtually since its inception three decades ago. He now serves as the publication's editor in chief and is co-host of *North American Whitetail Television* on Sportsman Channel.

In addition to his magazine and television duties, Gordon has contributed to a number of books, including the *Legendary Whitetails* series. He authored *World Record Whitetails: A Complete History of the No. 1 Bucks of All Time* and with noted researcher Dr. James Kroll co-authored *The Art & Science of Patterning Whitetails*. Gordon also has served as a frequent instructor at North American Whitetail University, a unique three-day short course on deer hunting and management.

A whitetail hunter since age five in his native Texas, Gordon has hunted the species in more than 40 states and provinces from Canada to Mexico, as well as in New Zealand and Finland. When he isn't hunting trophy bucks or producing media content about them, he enjoys spending time with his family at home in Marietta, Georgia.

Acknowledgments
Boone and Crockett Club's Complete Guide to Hunting Whitetails

A special thanks to the following individuals who graciously volunteered their time, talents, and/or photography to put this volume together:

René R. Barrientos
Craig Boddington
Heath Dreger
Richard T. Hale
Ken Hayworth
Glen Salow
Becca Spring
Larry Weishuhn
Bill Winke
Gordon Whittington

Additionally, we would like to recognize the following people for providing valuable content to *Boone and Crockett Club's Complete Guide to Hunting Whitetails*:

Denver Bryan
Dallen Lambson
Sandy Poston
Jack Reneau
Dave Richards
Len Rue, Jr.
Karlie Slayer
Justin Spring

Copyediting by
Julie Cowan of Cowan Creative

Printed and Bound by
Sheridan Books, Inc. located in Ann Arbor, Michigan

Boone and Crockett Club's Complete Guide to Hunting Whitetails
was design and produced by Julie L. Tripp, B&C Director of Publications,
using Adobe Creative Cloud software and featuring Franklin Gothic,
Garamond Premier Pro and Impact typefaces.